TRUST YOUR GUT

TRUST YOUR GUT

Residential Construction Contracts 101

KARALYNN CROMEENS

COPYRIGHT © 2025 KARALYNN CROMEENS
All rights reserved.

TRUST YOUR GUT
Residential Construction Contracts 101

FIRST EDITION

ISBN 978-1-5445-4750-3   *Hardcover*
     978-1-5445-4749-7   *Paperback*
     978-1-5445-4751-0   *Ebook*
     978-1-5445-4748-0   *Audiobook*

To my incredible team—Jess, Amanda, Kiara, and Jennifer—the ones who always figure out the "how" to my "why." Thank you for your hard work, your creative ideas, and for believing in me every step of the way.

CONTENTS

DISCLAIMER 9
INTRODUCTION 11
1. WHY YOU NEED A WRITTEN CONTRACT 21
2. TRUST YOUR GUT 35
3. NO LEGALESE REQUIRED 53
4. SCOPE OF WORK 61
5. CHANGE ORDERS 71
6. ESCAPE CLAUSE 85
7. PAYMENT TERMS 99
8. PROJECT SCHEDULE 115
9. PLAN FOR THE UNEXPECTED 127
10. CANCELLATION CLAUSE 137
11. STANDARDS 145
12. WARRANTIES 153
13. DISPUTES 163
14. ADDITIONAL PROVISIONS 179
15. PUNCH-OUT PROCESS 193
16. BONUS CHAPTER: CONTRACTS WITH SUBS 203
CONCLUSION 213
ABOUT THE AUTHOR 217

DISCLAIMER

Names and events in the stories found herein are based on true people, but details have been changed to protect their identities. Every lesson, however, is real.

Laws are always evolving, and while every effort is made to keep this publication updated as of its publishing date, I cannot guarantee the accuracy or outcomes related to the information presented in this book. I also do not assume any responsibility for claims, losses, or damages resulting from its use. Readers should not depend on this book for professional guidance.

This book and any related materials offer general insights into legal matters concerning residential construction. It is important to note that this text does not constitute legal advice, and nothing within it should be interpreted as such. Legal counsel should be sought from a licensed attorney. This book does not establish any enforceable rights. Readers are strongly encouraged to perform their own research regarding the laws and timelines applicable to their state. Please consult with a qualified attorney in your jurisdiction about your specific situation.

INTRODUCTION

Jacob's got a problem, and if you're a residential contractor, it's probably one you've faced, too.

He's been in the business for a few years, working hard, putting in the long hours, and dealing with the usual headaches that come with construction. But lately, those headaches have turned into full-blown anxiety. He's got a couple of clients who are threatening to sue over work they're not happy with, and Jacob feels like he's sitting on a ticking time bomb.

He's got a contract, sure, but it's technically not *his*—it's a patchwork template he copied from his last employer. It's incomplete, full of holes, and frankly, doesn't give him the kind of protection he needs. Now, with angry clients breathing down his neck, Jacob is starting to realize just how exposed he is. He can't sleep. He's stressed out, thinking about what will happen to his business, his reputation, and his family's livelihood if this thing blows up.

He tried looking to the internet for help and guidance, but couldn't find anything useful. Every time he searches online, he gets bombarded with confusing legal jargon and one-size-fits-all advice that doesn't apply to his business. His local attorney is decent, but doesn't specialize in construction law, so that's been a dead end as well.

Jacob feels like he's drowning.

He's overwhelmed by all this legal stuff, and the thought of sorting through it is exhausting. He's scared, he's tired, and he doesn't know where to start.

CONTRACTOR NIGHTMARES

I'm sure you can relate to Jacob. You've probably had those sleepless nights, staring at the ceiling, sweating over what might go wrong next, too. Maybe you don't have a contract in place, or like Jacob, you're using one you borrowed from some other guy and have no idea if it's worth the paper it's printed on. Perhaps you're currently knee-deep in a mess with a homeowner who's threatening to sue because something went wrong on the job.

None of these scenarios are ideal. In fact, I don't wish them upon any contractor. Luckily, there's something you can put into place to avoid them all: a solid contract.

I get it—contracts are boring as hell, but they're absolutely vital in the residential construction business.

A solid contract keeps your ass covered. It won't magically prevent every problem, but it will give you a fighting chance when things go sideways. With a proper contract in place, you can rest easy knowing you've got some armor on—even if it's not full-body armor.

A good contract isn't just a legal document—it's your safety net. It sets clear expectations, defines what's supposed to happen, and protects you when things go off the rails. It's peace of mind in written form, letting you get through your day without stressing about all the ways things could blow up.

Because let's face it, no one goes into this business to spend their time in court or chasing down payments. When you have a contract that covers all the bases, you can finally get some decent sleep, knowing you're less likely to get sucker-punched by a surprise lawsuit or an unpaid bill.

Plus, with a solid written contract, you'll find that things run smoother, your clients are less likely to throw tantrums, and you'll get to do what you're actually good at—building things.

WHAT YOU'LL LEARN IN THIS BOOK

By the time you've finished reading, you'll have the knowledge and confidence to draft a contract that *actually* protects your business—one that covers all the essentials and keeps you safe, without being bogged down by intimidating, hard-to-understand legalese. You'll learn exactly what needs to be included to cover your bases, avoid common pitfalls, and make sure you get paid for your work.

Each chapter breaks down the essentials of a residential construction contract, giving you the guidance you need to draft contracts that work for you. So, when it's time to put pen to paper, you'll know exactly what you're doing.

In the pages that follow, we'll cover the following:

- **Why You Need a Written Contract:** How clear contracts set expectations and cover your ass (CYA).
- **Trust Your Gut:** Why your instincts matter as much as your tools when picking clients.
- **No Legalese Required:** How you can write a contract with clear language.

- **Scope of Work:** How to define the job clearly so nobody can say, "I thought you were going to do that."
- **Change Orders:** The crucial process to document how the project changes.
- **Escape Clause:** How to exit your contract legally when things go south.
- **Payment Terms:** Setting up clear rules to make sure you get your money without the hassle.
- **Project Schedule:** Managing time frames so you're not stuck explaining why a three-month job is now at six.
- **Plan for the Unexpected:** Protecting yourself from curveballs that could throw your project off balance.
- **Cancellation Clause:** Ensuring you're compensated if the client bails halfway through.
- **Standards:** Clarifying what "good enough" looks like so everyone's on the same page.
- **Warranties:** Including the right kind of warranties to make sure you get paid in full before fixing anything.
- **Disputes:** How to prepare for when, not if, disagreements happen, so you can handle them like a pro.
- **Additional Provisions:** Extra clauses that save you headaches, from social media shares to pet safety.
- **Punch-Out Process:** How to finish strong, avoid endless tweaks, and secure that final payment.
- **Bonus Chapter: Contracts with Subs:** Why separate agreements with your subs are crucial to running a tight ship.

But more than learning how to write your contract, this book will teach you that a contract isn't just a defense mechanism—it's a tool for building better relationships with your clients.

By laying out clear expectations from the start, you can prevent many of the misunderstandings and disputes that lead to frustration and headaches in the first place.

In short, this book will empower you to *Trust Your Gut* and take control. You'll know how to protect your business, your future, and your peace of mind, all while creating a smoother, more positive experience for your clients.

WHY I WROTE THIS BOOK

I grew up in construction. My grandfather was an excavation contractor, and he built golf courses (the man was basically a dirt-moving legend). My brother and uncles are in the business, too—one's an electrician, another runs his own shop.

My first jobs were working for my uncle's irrigation business, where I learned pretty quickly that running a small construction business is about a lot more than just doing the work. It's dealing with every headache under the sun, from impossible clients to busted equipment to praying you have enough to cover payroll. I've seen it all, from projects going smooth as butter to the kind of disasters that make you want to crawl under a rock.

While I grew up with this stuff, I headed in a different direction: I pursued a law degree. In my last year of law school, however, life had other plans. My husband and I started our own material-supply business called Morrell Masonry Supply, and suddenly, all that legal knowledge I was cramming in school turned into real-world problems I had to solve—and fast.

Let me tell you, trying to juggle running a business, being its lawyer, and not losing your mind is an Olympic sport. But I got damn good at it. I graduated law school in 2004, and after a brief stint working for my real estate professor, I realized I needed to focus on helping businesses like ours. Morrell Masonry Supply was my first client, and I was its lawyer, manager, collections agent, you name it. I handled everything because I knew the pain points: the money fights, the confusing contracts, and the constant stress of keeping things running.

What I learned was that contractors aren't just missing tools, they're missing confidence. They're out there busting their asses, building things, and yet the paperwork side leaves them legally exposed. I've seen firsthand how unprotected they can be, so I made it my mission to change that. I built my business around small to midsize family contractors, helping them avoid the pitfalls that come with not having the right contracts.

I wrote my first book, *Quit Getting Screwed,* to help contractors understand commercial contracts. It wasn't until that book took off that I realized there was a huge gap for residential contractors. As a result, I spent COVID-19 digging into the contract rules across all fifty states, and my team and I developed a system that gets contractors what they need quickly and affordably.

And that's why I wrote this book: to help contractors like you. This book is your crash course in building a contract that protects you, lets you sleep at night, and keeps your business from turning into a circus.

But allow me to be clear—this book isn't going to magically make every job run like a dream. You're still going to have tough clients, delays, and headaches—that's simply the nature of construction. But this book will help you set things up so those issues don't sink your business.

This book is not going to turn an angry homeowner into your new best friend, and it won't guarantee you get paid every single time, either. But it will give you the tools to avoid a lot of the common traps contractors fall into and, hopefully, make your life a hell of a lot easier.

If you're ready to learn why you need a contract and what to include to protect your business, then let's dive in. We'll explore why exactly you need a contract in the next chapter.

CHAPTER 1

WHY YOU NEED A WRITTEN CONTRACT

In the world of construction, a handshake won't hold up a wall—only a well-written contract can.

Carl, a masonry contractor and client of mine, landed a job on a residential home doing stone and stucco work. As someone who usually worked as a subcontractor, this was his first time working directly with homeowners—and he couldn't be more excited.

The project looked promising and Carl was thrilled to put his skills to good use in Mr. and Mrs. Sarlo's home. After meeting with the homeowners, he created a mockup of how the finished project would look. The couple approved, and after receiving his first payment, Carl got to work.

As Carl made progress, issues cropped up—the kind you'd expect on any construction site. There were holes in the stonework, gaps with missing mortar, and cracks in the stucco. While this was normal for Carl, it was not normal for the Sarlos. They viewed his work as incomplete and sloppy. Instead of saying anything, however, they remained silent. Days turned into weeks, and their frustration grew as none of the imperfections were being fixed.

Eventually, they'd had enough and one day, Mr. Sarlo fired Carl for his subpar work.

Carl, flabbergasted, didn't understand. Didn't they know this was part of the process and that the very minor things they weren't happy about would be addressed later toward the end? Carl tried explaining but it was too late; the Sarlos couldn't see past their frustration.

A few weeks later, Carl received more bad news: Mr. and Mrs. Sarlo were suing him for everything they had paid him—$30,000—plus further damages.

Carl's heart sank. He called me to discuss options.

"Did you sign a contract?" I asked him.

"Umm, no, not officially," he said. "I drew a mockup and we agreed to payment terms after a handshake—that's it."

The case went to trial and Carl faced a jury. People tend to like jury trials because they're made up of people like us—which is true. But what are the chances of the jury being made up of construction workers? Not very high. What are the chances, on the other hand, of the jury being made up of homeowners?

You know the answer.

The jury saw photos of unfinished stonework and stucco cracks. As homeowners, they put themselves in Mr. and Mrs. Sarlo's shoes—not Carl's. And because none of them had background in construction, the jury also didn't understand that these were typical mid-project issues.

The evidence—including not having a signed contract—was damning, and the jury ruled against Carl, ordering him to repay everything he'd been paid, plus an additional $30,000 for corrections and their attorney's fees. It was a hefty sum that could have largely been avoided if Carl had a written (and signed!) contract.

In this chapter, you'll learn why you need a *written* contract and how it serves two main purposes: to properly manage expectations and to cover your ass (CYA).

RESIDENTIAL CONTRACTS 101

You'd think having a written contract is obvious, but it's easy to get caught up in conversations and agree to work with a simple handshake and mockup, like Carl did. When it comes to representing you in a court of law, however, having a signed document you can reference is critical.

I cannot emphasize this point enough: You *must* have a written contract for *every* project. Without one, there's really not much a lawyer can do for you in a court of law.

A written contract serves two purposes. The first purpose is to manage expectations throughout the entire process. The second is to CYA.

Let's get into both.

MANAGING EXPECTATIONS

The number one reason contractors get into trouble is because they failed to manage expectations. While you are an expert in your given field, you must also learn how to manage your clients.

Having a written contract is the best way to manage expectations. Every chapter in this book highlights one section of what you should include in your contract, but they all have one theme in common: managing expectations.

But having a well-written contract is only one part of the process.

You can have the best-of-the-best contract on paper, but if your client doesn't read or fully understand it, it won't do you any good. And let's be honest, clients rarely read the entire contract before signing. Knowing this, you need to take the time to verbally go over certain sections of the contract with your homeowner so both of you know what to expect during the process.

Managing expectations is about educating your client on the world of construction. It allows you to teach them how things work. No one likes surprises, especially when it comes to their home and their wallets. Taking the extra time to explain how the project is expected to pan out is time well spent.

If Carl had a written contract that included an explanation of a punch-out process, for example—and took the time to verbally explain what the process looks like to Mr. and Mrs. Sarlo—he could have avoided the frustration and eventual lawsuit filed against him.

The majority of homeowners are not construction professionals, and therefore have no idea how construction projects work. Most homeowners have a story they tell themselves about their project and how it's supposed to go. I don't have to tell you that their story is almost always wildly different from your picture of reality. In fact, many of them have false ideas of how things are built, how much they cost, and how much time they take—and we can blame home construction shows for that! Home remodel shows on TV often portray an inaccurate picture of how the construction world works, infusing many homeowners with unreal expectations.

Without engaging and setting expectations, the contractor goes into a project with the mindset that the homeowner thinks the same way he does, and the homeowner goes in with the mindset thinking that the contractor thinks the way he does. This is rarely the case.

To top things off, construction is an inherently stressful process.

Every project is unpredictable. As much as you try to predict everything, you simply can't. If you talk to married couples who have embarked on a home remodel project, the majority of them say, "We almost ended up in divorce over this project!" Just as marriages are imperfect, so are construction sites. It's hard enough to do it with someone you're married to, and as a contractor, you're like the third wheel.

That's why it is essential to be upfront with a homeowner and manage expectations every step of the way—and a written contract is the best way to do that.

WHY MANAGE EXPECTATIONS?

The primary reason for managing expectations is to prevent disputes down the line and avoid legal battles. While a written contract can't guarantee 100 percent protection against litigation, most of the cases I've encountered stem from poor management of expectations. This includes issues related to project timelines, visual outcomes, and communication gaps with homeowners.

Residential construction differs from commercial work because it involves people's homes—a deeply personal space. When someone's home is at stake, emotions run high, and conflicts are more likely to escalate. Unlike commercial contracts where clients leave the premises at the end of the day, residential projects occur within the homeowner's sanctuary.

This sanctuary represents security and safety, often their largest life investment. You're working in their living space, and they're present throughout the process. If something goes wrong, it's right in front of them, and their world crumbles.

Even when clients are in the wrong, emotions prevail. A seemingly minor mistake can overshadow an otherwise flawless project. As unfortunate as it is, homeowners tend to forget the 90 percent you got right and focus on that 10 percent hiccup. You'll go from their favorite person to the worst in the world. As professionals, we can't control how others behave, but we can manage our own actions.

Expectation management lies squarely within our control.

And when a homeowner expresses dissatisfaction, do not ignore it. Address complaints promptly and follow up with an email documenting the conversation and solution. Do not stick your head in the sand thinking it will go away—because it will not. It'll only get worse.

We'll explore more around disputes in Chapter 13.

CONTRACT LANGUAGE

Contrary to popular belief, your contract does not have to be complicated.

Contracts do not have to be full of hard-to-read, legalese language. In fact, I encourage you to do the opposite!

Write everything in plain English. Use the best language that clearly conveys your process. Make your contract straightforward and so easy to read, a ten year old could understand it.

You can also include whatever you want in your contract. While every state does require some specific language, the rest of your contract is in your control.

Be familiar with your contract. Whatever you include, you should understand every sentence and why it's there. Don't hire a lawyer to create a contract on your behalf and then not read it. Don't add language because your lawyer told you to without understanding the meaning behind it, either.

When you thoroughly understand your contract, you'll be able to confidently field any question from clients. This not only showcases your expertise but also ensures a high-quality experience for homeowners.

We'll cover more on contract language and state requirements in Chapter 3.

COVER YOUR ASS

While this may not be a legal term in court, cover your ass (CYA) means to protect yourself from getting sued.

Having a contract doesn't guarantee that you won't get sued, but it 100 percent helps cover your ass in the case that you do.

The chapters in this book represent important provisions based on experience, but in no way is this a complete list of provisions you should include in your contract. Each chapter represents a case (or several cases) I've represented in court and how my team and I created language or implemented strategies that worked to protect contractors.

Despite this list, an element of CYA lands on *you* and *your* experience as a contractor.

If something did not work well during one of your prior projects, it's your job to include a provision in your contract addressing that issue. Whatever hiccup, mistake, or challenge you've encountered needs to go in your contract, worded in a way to avoid what got you into trouble. You should be thinking about these during every job and updating your contract based on your experience.

Your contract is a living and breathing document. Revisit (and update) it often. We'll explore more additional provisions in Chapter 14.

Limiting your liability is another component of CYA. If

things go south, what's your maximum exposure? The point of a contract isn't so that no one sues you. The point of a contract is to limit the damages when they do. Simply knowing what your maximum exposure looks like on each project is a good way of covering your ass.

Carl could have set a limitation on damages in a contract that said he could "never be liable for more than what he's paid for." In his case, that would have limited his damages to the $30,000 he was paid and their attorney's fees. Without this language in a contract, however, the sky's the limit.

And lastly, while covering your ass is a way to protect yourself, and your time, from incurring damages, it also protects you from losing your license.

For example, in California, among other states, if you're a licensed contractor and you *don't* have a contract, you're not entitled to get paid. This is important to note because potentially sneaky people could use this against you. If someone hired you without a contract, and you went and completed the entire project, you'd risk not getting paid. You would have done all that work for free, and there would be nothing that you could do about it.

Thankfully, most states that have a licensing requirement require some type of contract.

> **KEY TAKEAWAYS**
>
> - You need a *written* contract.
> - The contract should be in plain English.
> - Take the time to walk your customer through the contract.
> - The purpose of your written contract is to manage expectations and CYA.
> - A contract is a promise—if you break your promise it is a breach of the contract.

SLEEP BETTER AT NIGHT

I have been in construction litigation for nearly twenty years. I have represented both contractors and homeowners, and most of the litigation could have been prevented if the homeowner's expectations had been properly managed.

When you have a signed written contract, you can sleep better at night, knowing that even if something does go wrong, you're protected as much as possible.

If Carl had a signed contract that detailed the punch-out process, I could have shown the jury what both parties had agreed to, and that the homeowners didn't give us a chance to get to this crucial part of the process. I could have explained that we had it built into the agreement, but that Mr. and Mrs. Sarlo didn't even let Carl get that far.

Of course, a contract can't protect you from everything—especially if you're dealing with a client who's throwing up red flags from the start. If that's the case, save yourself and don't work with them. Before you sign any contract, be sure to trust your gut, which we'll cover in the next chapter.

CHAPTER 2

TRUST YOUR GUT

Ninety percent of the contractors who end up in my office after getting sued tell me the same thing:

"I didn't like this guy from day one."

"I knew something was off with this couple."

"I felt off about this project from the start."

Many contractors end up in lengthy and costly lawsuits with homeowners who they had a bad feeling about in the early stages, but they took the job anyway.

In other words, they ignored their gut.

This chapter is all about trusting your gut, because even

the best contract won't prevent getting sued. Trusting your instincts is just as important—if not more—as your written contracts. While a contract can certainly help protect you in a court of law, it does not prevent lawsuits from happening in the first place.

Do you know what prevents lawsuits from happening in the first place? When you listen to your gut and avoid working with troublesome clients from the start.

The purpose of this chapter is to give yourself permission to trust your gut *before* signing a contract. When it comes to working with potential homeowners, listen to your intuition to avoid headaches during the build process and potential lawsuits from litigious-prone people.

In this chapter, we'll cover some common red flags to look out for when engaging with potential clients. We'll then cover tips and strategies that will give enough time for you to trust your gut about a new client.

If only my client Mark had trusted his gut before signing on a home-build project.

HIGH MAINTENANCE HOMEOWNERS

In the heart of Minnesota, where pristine lakes mirror the sky, our home builder found himself meeting with a couple who wanted to build their dream house on a plot of land next to a beautiful lake.

From the outset, before the contract was signed, Mark sensed trouble brewing. The homeowners, Mr. and Mrs. Harrington, exuded an air of entitlement that made every interaction feel like a test of his patience. They were extremely high maintenance, demanding more time and attention than seemed reasonable. They insisted that Mark come to their house in person, not just once but multiple times, to answer questions they could have easily asked over the phone. They pushed him to meet with their architect—before any contract was signed—as if his expertise was theirs to command for free.

And it didn't stop there. They even floated the idea of having him submit for the permit on their behalf, again without so much as a written agreement. It was clear they wanted all the benefits of his work and time without committing to anything in return. To top it off, they casually mentioned they were shopping around, talking to other contractors who, in their words, "might be able to do it cheaper." This wasn't just a red flag—it was a whole parade of warning signs waving frantically in front of him.

I don't have a great feeling about this, Mark thought to himself.

This wasn't his first rodeo, however. Mark knew he could manage expectations and have a solid contract, even with high maintenance homeowners. The project was big, which factored heavily in his decision to proceed. Both parties signed the contract.

It didn't take long, but the Harringtons' demands escalated. They wanted more, faster, better. They complained about the noise, the trash, and the workers. They pointed out the tiniest of flaws, and asked about the timeline every morning. Even though with each milestone, Mark and his team's craftsmanship was impeccable, the Harringtons' expectations knew no bounds.

Eventually, Mark had had enough and told Mr. and Mrs. Harrington that he was done. "I quit!" He had an escape clause in his contract (more on this in Chapter 6), so he felt comfortable walking away from the project. For Mark, it just wasn't worth all the extra requests, the emotional toll, the extra time it took to manage their every need. He was over it.

To his surprise, the Harringtons pleaded for him to stay. "We're sorry," they said. "We'll lay off. We really appreciate your work and will make less of a fuss about everything."

The project was close to completion—just some landscaping to finish—and Mark thought about those final payments on such a big project. He accepted their apology and gave them a second chance. He decided to stick it out to the end.

And then the hammer fell—a lawsuit. The Harringtons accused Mark of subpar landscaping, demanding $80,000.

"Damn it," he said to me. "I should have listened to my gut."

"You should have, indeed," I said.

In the end, Mark settled, paying half the sum to avoid a lengthy court process. He wanted to officially close this project out and move on—vowing to never ignore his gut again.

RED FLAGS

Mr. and Mrs. Harrington were overly demanding before the contract was signed, which was a red flag for Mark, but he decided to ignore his gut and continue working with the troublesome couple anyway.

The following represent some common red flags you should look out for. These warning signs can help you avoid costly mistakes down the line.

1. A HOMEOWNER PRESENTS YOU WITH THEIR OWN CONTRACT

No one knows your business or your expertise better than you. In no way would it be appropriate for a client to expect you to sign a building contract that they (the non-expert) give to you. Please say no.

2. A HOMEOWNER WANTS TO CHANGE THE CONTRACT AFTER IT'S BEEN SIGNED

I encountered a situation with a contractor—we'll call him Hugo—where he had a signed contract with a homeowner who paid the deposit. Everything seemed on track for the work to begin, but on the day the project was set to start, the client dropped a bombshell: "We're not going to pay you upfront before each milestone. I'll pay you once the work is completed instead."

This was contrary to the agreed-upon terms set out in the already signed contract.

Hugo called me from the homeowner's front yard. "What should I do?" he asked. I advised him honestly: "The client isn't honoring the contract he signed, so you have two choices: accept his new terms or walk away."

Hugo decided to walk away—a wise move. The homeowner eventually hired someone else, and Hugo avoided a potential nightmare. Because his contract stipulated that deposits were nonrefundable, Hugo retained the $10,000 deposit the homeowner paid to start the project.

If a client wants to rewrite your contract or change it after it's been signed, that's a red flag. In Hugo's case, because his payment terms were different in his contract and the homeowner wanted to change the terms afterward, he walked away from the project with no issues (more on payment terms in Chapter 7).

3. A HOMEOWNER TRIES TO BEAT YOU DOWN ON PRICE

This behavior reveals their attitude toward your work, which means they don't value you. Again, you are the expert in your work and you know what things cost, so stick to your numbers.

I'd also like to add that consistency sets the tone for your working relationship with each homeowner. Deviating from your numbers could make it appear that you are indecisive or that you're overcharging. The thought for the homeowner then becomes, "If he overcharged me here and lowered the cost for me, then that means he's overcharging me everywhere and I need to fight to lower every cost."

You can imagine the fun you'd have dealing with this client on your project.

If a client tries to beat you down on price by showing you the price he was quoted from another builder, that is a red flag, and I would tell the homeowner to go with that builder then.

4. THEY TREAT YOU LIKE MERE HELP AND NOT AN EXPERT

Too often, homeowners view contractors as mere "help," an extension of the tools they wield. In this skewed perspective, the value of your expertise, your sweat, and your craftsmanship diminishes, and it will show up in the way they treat you throughout the entire project. You deserve better. Recognize your worth. You're more than a tool—you are an expert in your field. Homeowners should see you for what you truly are: a partner. If they don't, then move on.

5. A HOMEOWNER IS OVERLY DEMANDING AND YOU HAVE NOT AGREED TO WORK FOR THEM YET

The Harringtons were pushy and expected Mark to do a lot before he even signed the contract—far more than what any reasonable homeowner would ask. They treated the pre-contract phase as though Mark was already on their payroll, pushing him to meet their architect for design discussions, answer endless rounds of questions in person, and provide detailed input on their project timeline. They even floated the audacious request for Mark to begin the permit application process before anything was finalized, as if his time and expertise came with no strings attached. It became increasingly clear they wanted him to invest significant effort upfront, without offering any assurance they would ultimately choose him for the job. For Mark, it felt less like securing a potential client and more like being strung along as their unpaid consultant.

Over-demanding clients usually have unrealistic expectations and they are hard to please. Pushiness from clients is often a sign that they don't trust your expertise—perhaps thinking they could do better. These are all red flags. For contractors, first impressions matter. It's like going on a date with someone for the first time. If you're already sensing unattractive qualities, those qualities aren't going to go away. In fact, they usually get worse! Some projects, like ill-fated romances, don't improve with time. If you're seeing behavior problems from homeowners before the contract is even signed, I would not take on the project.

6. A HOMEOWNER ASKS YOU TO NOT PULL PERMITS

If a homeowner asks you to not pull a permit, don't listen to them! This is a huge red flag. Even if you get along with this client, even if you want to be a good sport, even if you need the money, if they're asking you to do something that puts your license on the line, don't do it.

7. A HOMEOWNER WANTS TO CHANGE YOUR PROCESS

On occasion, some homeowners are bold enough to try and change your process to suit them. As the expert, you should be very wary when this happens and look at the request with keen eyes. If the requested change enhances your process, then that is surely something for you to mull over and decide later. But if it doesn't, then push back on the request and stick to your tried-and-true process.

If you do change your process for a client, be sure to cover your ass and update your contract to reflect the new changes. A client of mine failed to do this and learned this lesson the hard way. Summit Ridge Homes, a seasoned company that builds homes, decided not only to ignore their gut, but also to go completely off-process for a homeowner.

As you'd expect, things did not end well.

As a home builder, Summit Ridge Homes' business model is based on the homeowner picking out the design of their home, but then leaving Summit Ridge to do all the work building it. Their marketing includes language like, "From the biggest decisions to the smallest details, our specialists offer you the freedom to personalize floor plans, finish work, and colors so you can build a home that is unique to your family."

One homeowner—we'll call him Nathaniel—decided to take this marketing message to the next level: he wanted the freedom to hire subcontractors directly. Nathaniel had friends in the field and wanted to hire them to build his dream home.

Gary, who I represented in this case, typically worked as the construction manager for Summit Ridge and their projects. With their typical process, Gary oversaw every aspect of home construction. After receiving Nathaniel's request, however, Gary wanted to live up to the Summit Ridge Homes marketing promise, so he agreed to give Nathaniel the freedom to personalize this home-build experience.

Instead of Gary hiring subcontractors per Summit Ridge's standard policy and procedures, Nathaniel would hire them out and pay them directly.

Gary, unfortunately, did not update the contract to detail this change in procedure. Gary still acted like a construction manager, but without a construction manager contract.

While Nathaniel hired the subs and paid them, Gary still managed the symphony of builders, electricians, and plumbers and made sure the build was on track. Throughout the process, Nathaniel paid the subs directly, bypassing the traditional channels. Things went well—until the roof job.

The roofer's work fell short of Nathaniel's expectations. The roof sagged in one area and rain tiptoed through the gaps. Nathaniel, displeased, withheld payment. But here's the twist: Gary had hired the roofer, albeit informally. His name graced the roofer's contract.

"You hired them," Nathaniel declared, "so you pay them."

Gary and Summit Ridge found themselves facing a $30,000 lawsuit. In their defense, we tried to explain that they were merely the construction manager, not the payer of subs, as requested by the homeowner. The absence of a formal contract detailing the agreement with the homeowner, however, left Gary and Summit Ridge Homes vulnerable.

This case went to court and the judge weighed the evidence: the unsigned contract, the unpaid roofer, and the tangled web of responsibilities. In the end, justice tilted toward the homeowner. Summit Ridge, despite its noble intentions, had to pay.

Summit Ridge Homes had a strict process in place and they should have stuck to it. Nathaniel asking to go off-process should have been a red flag. If they stuck to their process, they could have avoided the entire debacle.

TIPS & STRATEGIES

While you want to avoid the red flags, here are some tips for uncovering them:

1. MEET BOTH SPOUSES

When working on a project involving a home owned by a married couple, it's essential to meet with both spouses. Here's why.

Firstly, marital issues can impact the project. If the couple is going through difficulties, it might affect their decision-making or communication during the process. By meeting both parties, you gain insight into their relationship dynamic, allowing you to navigate potential challenges more effectively.

Secondly, even if there are no immediate issues, involving both spouses from the start is crucial. Sometimes, one spouse may not be initially engaged in the project, but they might later express dissatisfaction or surprise if they're left out of the loop. Ensuring both are informed and on board helps prevent misunderstandings down the line.

Meeting both spouses provides valuable context and helps establish clear communication throughout the project.

2. INTRODUCE A DESIGN CONTRACT FIRST

When advising sizable remodelers or new-home builders, I recommend a strategic approach: require a design contract first, followed by a build contract. This dual-step process serves two critical purposes.

First, it ensures fair compensation for the work performed, even at this stage. As contractors, many of you invest significant time and effort in design and pre-planning, hoping to secure the actual job. Unfortunately, you often go unpaid for these early and time-consuming stages. This design contract gets you paid for your time. More on this in Chapter 4.

Secondly, it allows you to collaborate closely with the

homeowner (or homeowners) to give you a sense of who they are before you sign the build contract.

Having a design contract allows you to test the waters with the client's personality. How will you work together? What's the dynamic like during meetings with designers and engineers? How responsive are they? How many revisions did they ask for? Were they pleasant or pushy? By the end of this phase, you can deliver what the client paid for and either part ways amicably or seamlessly transition to the build contract.

If compatibility issues arise during this initial stage, you can reconsider moving forward—even if you "need the work." This approach saves you from costly missteps down the road.

In other words, this process allows for enough time for you to trust your gut.

3. DON'T SIGN A BUILD CONTRACT UNTIL THE PERMITS ARE APPROVED.

Taking a step further, I also recommend securing permits before transitioning to the build stage. Why? Because until you have that permit in hand, you don't truly know what the job entails. Sure, you may have an agreed set of designs planned, but the permit process often changes them.

Because each of these stages can be stressful—the design iterations, responsiveness, and the sometimes lengthy permitting timeline—they give you a glimpse of how your client will behave during the building phase, which usually lasts much longer and entails more contact. How patient are they? Do they understand the process when you explain it to them? By factoring permit approval into your process, you'll mitigate risks and see if you truly want to work with this client.

This strategy allows enough time to see if a client is a good fit or not. If you didn't enjoy working with this homeowner during this phase, you don't have to continue working with them.

4. DON'T OVERRIDE YOUR GUT BECAUSE YOU NEED THE MONEY

Try not to override your gut feeling because money is tight and you need a project. I know financial stresses squeeze us mentally, making us more agreeable to clients because we feel like we need the money.

If you're seeing red flags with a potential client, and you absolutely need the job, then it is imperative for you to double down on managing expectations, covering your ass, and having a well-written contract (with all the provisions we're about to cover in the chapters that follow).

> **KEY TAKEAWAYS**
>
> - Trust your gut. If a client does not feel like a good fit, don't move forward.
> - If things are shaky in the beginning, they won't get better throughout the project.
> - If you see red flags, either don't take the job or manage expectations extra well.

DON'T IGNORE YOUR GUT

Don't be that 90 percent of my clients who ignored their gut, took the job, and then ended up paying for it down the line after all the work had already been done. Mark could have avoided a $40,000 settlement by not taking Mr. and Mrs. Harrington on as clients in the first place. They were overly demanding before the contract was signed—a red flag. Additionally, Mark could have walked away when he first grew tired of their behavior with his escape clause, but was then suckered back in again. He ignored his gut twice!

Similarly, if Gary from Summit Ridge Homes saw Nathaniel's request to hire subs on his own as a red flag, he could have stuck to their tried-and-true process and could have avoided their judgment in court to pay the roofer.

Keep an eye out for those red flags and be empowered

to say no to (or even fire) clients if they don't value you and your expertise.

As I mentioned in Chapter 1, you don't have to make the contract's language complicated. In fact, the more straightforward, the better! More on this in the next chapter.

CHAPTER 3

NO LEGALESE REQUIRED

"I'm not smart enough to write my own contract."

"I don't know what should go in there."

"It's too complicated."

"I'm not a good writer."

If I had $100 for every time I heard these excuses, I'd be on a yacht right now.

Unfortunately, these thoughts leave many contractors stuck in limbo—paralyzed by the fear of writing their own contracts, and worse, operating without one altogether. Trust me, that's a disaster waiting to happen.

But here's the beautiful thing: Contracts don't need to be complicated. In fact, the best contracts are simple, clear, and easy for both you and your clients to understand. No legalese required! You don't have to be a lawyer or a "good writer" to create a contract that protects your business—you just need a bit of guidance, which is exactly what this chapter is about.

DON'T LET THE LEGAL JARGON SCARE YOU

The biggest mistake contractors make is thinking that a contract has to be filled with fancy legal terms to be effective. That couldn't be further from the truth. The purpose of a contract is to manage expectations—yours and your client's. You can't do that if no one can understand what the contract says!

There's no magic potion for making a contract effective. It doesn't need to say "heretofore" or "party of the first part." In fact, it's better if it doesn't. Plain language is the way to go. You don't need a law degree; you just need to write what's important to your business in a way you and your client can both understand.

Here's a bonus: Even if a homeowner doesn't physically sign the contract but pays you and you start work, the contract is still valid. By sending the payment and moving forward, they've agreed to your terms, whether or not they scrawled their signature on the dotted line. That said, some states require actual signatures on the contract to preserve your lien rights against the project—so it's always a good idea to double-check your state's requirements before moving forward.

DON'T SWEAT THE STATE REQUIREMENTS

Let's talk about state-specific requirements. Every state has some level of protection for homeowners built into their laws. Why? Because homeowners are considered less business-savvy than commercial clients and are seen as more vulnerable to being taken advantage of. That's why states step in with certain legal requirements for residential contracts.

One big thing most states require is language about **lien rights**. This is a legal right that allows contractors to claim a lien on a property if they aren't paid for their work. Another common requirement is listing your **contractor's license number** and whether you're **insured**. These are small details, but they can be important.

The good news? You can easily find out what your state requires by checking with your local licensing board. For example, in California, the Contractors State License Board (CSLB) provides a list of what needs to be in your contract. It's usually pretty straightforward, so don't let it intimidate you.

Most of the time, you're talking about technical requirements, like having your license number and insurance details in the contract—nothing huge. It's not hard to meet these standards once you know where to look. Just Google your state's licensing requirements, and you'll find what you need to include.

WHY BORROWING CONTRACTS IS A BAD IDEA

Let's talk about Dan. Dan was a contractor who didn't have his own contract, so he borrowed one from a buddy, thinking, *Hey, it's a contract—what could go wrong?* Well, a lot, as it turns out.

Dan had a job with a client, Lisa, to remodel her kitchen. Halfway through the project, Lisa stopped making payments. Dan figured no problem, the contract probably has a clause that allows him to stop working if he isn't paid. So he stopped work. That's when things went south.

Lisa fired Dan and hired another contractor, Bob, to finish the job. But Bob charged more than Dan's original quote, so Lisa sued Dan for the extra money she had to pay to complete the work.

Dan, confident that his borrowed contract would protect him, went to court. Unfortunately, Dan had never actually read the contract, and it didn't have the clause he thought it did. Even worse, the language that was there was so convoluted that no one could understand it, not even the judge. The contract didn't protect Dan at all. The court ruled that Dan was at fault, and he had to pay Lisa the difference between what he had charged and what she ended up paying Bob.

The moral of the story? Don't use a contract you don't understand. If you don't know what's in it, how can you expect it to protect you? That's why writing your own contract in plain language is so critical. It doesn't have to be full of legal jargon to be effective—it just has to be clear.

YOU CAN DO THIS: NO LAWYER NECESSARY

You don't need a lawyer to write a contract. I wrote this book so you *don't* have to spend thousands on a lawyer to create a contract for you. I've heard horror stories—like the guy who hired a lawyer to draft his contract and was quoted $1,500, only to receive the contract (and a bill for $8,000) three months later!

You don't need that kind of stress. With the right guidance, you can have a working contract in just a few days. It's not about fancy language; it's about clear communication. When your contract reflects how you do business, it's easy to explain to your clients, and it protects you in case things go south.

And when you write your own contract, you'll know exactly what it says! If a homeowner asks you about a specific clause, you won't have to scramble to check your contract—you'll be able to confidently explain it because you wrote it. You'll have the peace of mind knowing your contract is tailored to your business and meets your specific needs.

> **KEY TAKEAWAYS**
>
> - Contracts should be easy to read and understand to manage expectations.
> - Make sure you have your state requirements in there.
> - Be familiar with your own contract so you can answer questions confidently.

TAKE CONTROL OF YOUR CONTRACTS

Writing your own contract doesn't require a law degree or a mastery of legal jargon. All you need is clear, simple language that sets the expectations for both you and your clients. Don't be afraid to make your contract your own—it's there to protect your business.

Dan learned the hard way that using a contract you don't understand can lead to big problems. But you don't have to make that same mistake. By writing your own contract, you're in control, and you won't be caught off guard if a client asks a question or a dispute arises.

And most importantly, know that you can do this. Your contract doesn't have to be a scary legal document—it just needs to clearly communicate the terms of the agreement.

Once you feel good about writing your own contract, you can move on to the most important part: the scope of work, which we'll cover in the next chapter.

CHAPTER 4

SCOPE OF WORK

Many contractors I've worked with rely solely on a scope of work, thinking it's the same as having a contract.

Newsflash: They are not synonymous!

A contract should encompass much more than just the scope of work. While the scope of work is a crucial component, a comprehensive contract includes various provisions to ensure clarity and protect all parties involved—which I detail with each chapter of this book.

While I applaud my clients for at least having a scope of work as their contract, clarity was often missing—and that got them into trouble. For some, their scope of work wasn't detailed enough, leading to misunderstandings and disputes. For others, it wasn't clear, and the homeowner expected more than what was agreed upon.

In this chapter, we'll dive into what your scope of work should really look like. We'll explore how to make it comprehensive and clear, ensuring it protects you and sets the right expectations for your clients.

If only my client, Jake, understood this.

A COSTLY OVERSIGHT

In the sun-drenched heart of California, Jake, a diligent pool contractor, embarked on a project. The homeowner, Mrs. Lawson, envisioned a seamless connection between her new pool and the existing concrete sidewalk.

Unfortunately, Jake's scope of work didn't include this crucial detail.

As the pool took shape, Mrs. Lawson raised an eyebrow. "Where's the sidewalk connection?" she asked.

Jake hesitated, then confessed, "It wasn't in the original scope."

Mrs. Lawson's eyes narrowed. "What do you mean? But

they have to connect! It doesn't make sense if they don't connect!"

She was right. Jake weighed his options. Lawsuits loomed like storm clouds—especially in California—so he made a choice. He bridged the gap, poured concrete, and ensured continuity. Mrs. Lawson smiled, blissfully unaware of Jake's sacrifice.

While Jake avoided being sued, the oversight in his scope of work cost him $10,000, which, sadly, was more than what he made on the job.

SCOPE OF WORK

The scope of work is arguably the most important part of a residential construction contract. Without it, how would you know what to do? What does the homeowner want? How would you price the project? You can't answer these questions until you know what the job entails.

When creating a scope of work, the level of detail matters significantly. Some contractors opt for a high-level approach, providing a lump-sum price for the entire project—"I'll remodel your kitchen for $X." A much more effective and transparent approach, however, is itemizing the work.

Instead of merely stating the overall cost, I recommend breaking down the project into specific components. Let's take a kitchen remodel, for example. An itemized list would include details like cabinet installation, countertop materials, flooring, plumbing fixtures, electrical work, and so on. By doing this, you offer clarity to both parties—to yourself and to your client. This transparency fosters trust, minimizes misunderstandings, and ensures that everyone is on the same page regarding what's included in the project.

Are you sensing a theme here? It's all about setting those expectations!

When creating a scope of work, be as clear as possible. Pretend you're explaining what the job entails to a child who knows nothing about construction. The clearer you are, the better it will set expectations for the homeowner. Remember, homeowners have no frame of reference when it comes to the construction process and how homes are built. This is your chance to show them your expertise and offer an experience that is clear from the get-go.

If you don't have a scope of work and you get into a dispute, a judge or jury will decide what your scope of work was—and that's a very expensive fight. If a potential client comes to me wanting to sue, but they don't have a scope of work, I won't take the case because it is unlikely that we will succeed.

When it comes to disputes in court, without a scope of work, it becomes a matter of "he said, she said," relying solely on testimony. If your case reaches trial, the central question becomes: Who seems more trustworthy? This judgment rarely reflects the actual quality of the work done; instead, it centers on your character. Factors like how you communicate, your likability, and even how you dress can influence a judge's or jury's perception. More often than not, judges and juries lean toward homeowners, finding it easier to empathize with them than with contractors. So, in court, without a well-defined scope of work, it becomes a battle of credibility—deciding who is more believable based on these subjective factors.

Another thing I often hear clients complain about is not getting paid for work they've completed: "I did this work and I didn't get paid."

"Was it in your scope of work?" I always ask.

"Well, no. It was extra work that I did during the job."

I hate it when they give this answer.

"I can't really help you, bud. If the work wasn't clearly listed in your contract, you're shit out of luck."

If you complete work outside of the agreed upon scope of

work, you are not entitled to get paid for said work. If your client asks you to change anything outside of the agreed upon scope of work, you must submit a change order in order to get paid (more on this in the next chapter).

And lastly, it's important to specify what is *not* included in your scope of work. For example, if you're remodeling a kitchen, make it clear that the bathroom is not included. In the scope of work, include a line that states, "Anything not specifically included above is excluded."

This will cover you and ensure there are no misunderstandings.

A PROJECT LOST AFTER PERMITTING

A client of mine—we'll call him Albert—ran a construction company focused on backyard and front porch projects. His client, Mr. Morris, wanted a backyard oasis: a pool, a deck, and a pergola where laughter would echo. Albert listened, nodding as Mr. Morris's excitement spilled across the blueprint. They meticulously laid out the scope of work, and after hours putting the contract in place and explaining the details, they both signed.

Before Albert's crew could get to work, they applied for the necessary permits. Alex submitted the blueprints, and now they had to wait. Days stretched into weeks, and the phone stayed silent. No green light meant no shovel hitting soil.

Then the letter arrived—the municipality's verdict. Changes were mandatory. The pool's depth violated safety codes; the deck encroached on an easement. Albert's heart sank. The extra cost after changing the scope of work? An extra $50,000—a sum that mocked the original budget.

He met Mr. Morris, the blueprints spread across the same kitchen table. "We've hit a snag," Albert said, his voice apologetic. "The changes mean more work, more materials."

Mr. Morris's face fell. "But I can't afford this."

Albert understood, but he couldn't help feeling defeated. He'd put in countless hours up until this point. Unfortunately, the pool remained a blueprint; Mr. Morris couldn't move forward.

Albert considered legal battles—the signed contract, the fine print. But he didn't. He swallowed the pill and moved on.

PERMITS FIRST

If you are working on a project that requires a permit, you should require a design contract that goes through permitting *before* you put together a build contract. If you think about it, this is common sense: You won't know the exact scope of work until that permit is approved.

I briefly mentioned this approach in Chapter 2 and highlighted how this dual-step process helps you get to know a client before embarking on the longer-term build process.

I also mentioned a design contract ensures fair compensation for the time it takes to submit the necessary paperwork for permitting. This design process allows you to get paid for this crucial part of any build—nothing too outrageous, but enough to cover the back and forth with the designer and your multiple applications to get the project approved through permitting. I've seen clients charge a flat fee between $1,500 and $3,000 for their design contract, which is totally reasonable.

If Albert had charged Mr. Morris for a design contract first, not only would the permitting process accurately depict what his scope of work would be, he also could have been paid for the time he spent gathering information and submitting the paperwork for those permits.

Albert's experience highlights how a separate design contract is crucial. It doesn't have to be complicated, either. I view it as a mini contract before the physical part of a project starts. It should only be a few pages highlighting the scope of work during this stage: working with the designer to submit the proper paperwork for the permitting process.

Be sure to always set expectations (there's that theme again!). I've had clients get fired because the permitting process took six months as opposed to the ninety days depicted in their contract. Builders are not designers. We have no control over how long municipalities will take with their permitting. Being upfront and setting expectations about how you're not in control of the permit process is a part of covering your ass.

And lastly, as I also pointed out in Chapter 2, this process lets you test out working with the homeowner. You will have worked enough with this client to see if he is a good fit. If you don't get along, you can simply turn the entire project over to them and they can hire somebody else.

> **KEY TAKEAWAYS**
>
> - Without a scope of work, you don't know what's included in the project and what's not.
> - During a dispute in court, if you don't have a scope of work, a judge or jury will decide what it was for you—which is a position you never want to be in!
> - You are not entitled to get paid for work not included in the scope of work.
> - Don't work for free: Require a design contract in your process before you get to a build contract. This should be non-negotiable with projects that require a permit.

A BLUEPRINT FOR SUCCESS

A well-defined scope of work is your blueprint for success. It not only guides the project, but also protects you from potential disputes, misunderstandings, and unpaid work. It's about more than just spelling out the details; it's about setting expectations, ensuring clarity, and establishing trust from the outset. By taking the time to create a detailed scope of work, you're not just avoiding headaches—you're positioning yourself as a professional who values transparency and fairness.

Even if the scope of work might look perfect, construction isn't a perfect world. Things are bound to change—and that's okay. You've got a process in place to handle it, which is the focus of our next chapter.

CHAPTER 5

CHANGE ORDERS

I don't think I've ever heard of a project that didn't have a change order. They're pretty much guaranteed!

Once a contract is signed, it's a binding agreement. Any changes to that agreement need to be in writing and agreed upon by both parties. We call these modifications "change orders." Whether it's a minor tweak or a major adjustment, a change order is the official document that alters the original terms.

You know this.

I know this.

But does your homeowner?

I'm willing to bet a lot of money and say no, they do not.

In this chapter, I'll highlight how effectively managing change orders is crucial for you to maintain control of the project, protect your financial interests, and foster clear communication with your clients. By setting expectations early, documenting every change, and ensuring all parties understand the process, you can prevent misunderstandings, disputes, and financial losses.

BE THE EXPERT

Proactively explaining the change order process to homeowners sets you up for success. It shows that you know what you're doing, and when changes inevitably come up, it won't feel like a surprise. Without this upfront conversation, you risk losing credibility.

Trust me, nothing shakes a homeowner's confidence faster than a contractor springing unexpected changes on them.

Setting expectations is key to preserving that trust, and it starts long before the work begins. Even before they sign on the dotted line, let your client know that things are bound to change. The scope of work might look airtight, but construction isn't a perfect world—and that's okay, because you've got a process in place to handle it.

For example, be up front about the kinds of surprises that often arise in your line of work. Explain how a roofer might discover that some decking needs replacement once the shingles are removed, or how a remodeler might open a wall and find outdated electrical wiring that doesn't meet current codes. Homeowners need to hear that these issues are common and part of the reality of construction, but more importantly they need to know you've planned for them.

You could say something like, "These types of discoveries happen all the time. That's why we have a system in place to handle changes. If we run into anything unexpected, we'll issue a change order, review the costs together, and agree on how to move forward before we start any additional work."

Maybe your explanation sounds like this: "Hey, homeowner, in a perfect world, this scope of work would cover everything. But since we don't live in that world, here's our process for handling changes. If you want to modify anything, we'll issue a change order so it's all in writing. We'll both sign off, and if the change affects the cost, we'll include that in the change order as well. No new work starts until that payment is taken care of. Any questions?"

Clear communication from the start is critical, especially when it comes to legal documents like a contract. These days, it's easy to fire off a contract electronically and get a signature back, but that doesn't mean the homeowner has actually read it. In fact, they probably haven't. That's why it's always a good idea to sit down with your clients and go over key sections face-to-face. The best contractors do this because it establishes trust, clarifies expectations, and ultimately leads to a smoother project.

THE CHANGE ORDER PROCESS

Maybe you find something unexpected that needs fixing, or the homeowner suddenly decides they must have that custom built-in cabinet they saw on Pinterest. Whatever the reason, any time the project scope changes, you need a plan to handle it. That's where the trusty change order comes in.

Think of a change order as your "get-it-in-writing" insurance. It's a formal document that outlines any modifications to the original plan, whether it's adding something new, removing a piece of the project, or making a last-minute switch. If it changes the scope of work, it needs to be documented in a change order.

Here's how it usually goes down:

1. **Spotting the Change:** Let's say the homeowner wants to add a built-in cabinet to the living room.

First, we figure out how much it's going to cost and how it's going to impact the project timeline. (Because yeah, that cabinet might push back the whole project.)

2. **Putting It on Paper:** Next, we create a change order. This spells out everything—cost, any changes to the deadline, and the details of the new scope. If adding that fancy cabinet pushes the project back two weeks, we put that right in the change order.
3. **Getting the Green Light—and the Cash:** The golden rule here is that change orders get paid in full before you start the extra work. No exceptions. This keeps the cash flow smooth and avoids those awkward "But I thought this was included?" conversations down the line.
4. **Always, Always Get It in Writing:** Even if the homeowner verbally agrees to a change, never rely on a handshake or a friendly nod. If it's not in writing, you're not guaranteed to get paid. And believe me, this happens all the time. A homeowner might tell you, "Oh yeah, I'll pay for that at the end of the project," but when you submit the final bill, they suddenly have amnesia. A signed change order eliminates all of that.

A change order isn't just for adding things—it's also for taking stuff out. Say the homeowner decides to skip the new appliances. That's fine, but you still need a change order that reflects the reduced cost. This keeps the budget clear and makes sure everyone's on the same page—no need for guessing games.

Nothing is too trivial to document. Whether it's a major upgrade or a small tweak, get it in writing and have it signed. Not only does this help avoid confusion, but it protects you if a dispute pops up later (more on disputes in Chapter 13).

Another valuable tip? Consider charging a fee for submitting change orders—especially when you're working with clients who can't seem to make up their minds. Change orders take time to prepare, and that time is worth something. Just having the option of a fee gives you leverage. You don't always have to enforce it, but it's good to have in your contract for those clients who might start making a habit out of adding new requests.

Every change, no matter how small or insignificant it may seem, needs to be documented. Create the change order, make copies, and attach them to the scope of work. Once signed, both you and the homeowner get copies to ensure everyone knows what's going on. This attention to detail keeps your project organized and prevents misunderstandings from snowballing into larger conflicts.

DON'T WORK FOR FREE

There's a time and place for charity, but a construction contract isn't one of them. If you don't use change orders, you might as well be working for free—and that's not the business you're in.

At the end of the day, the rule is simple: If you want to get paid, write it down. And get it signed. No paperwork, no payment—it's as easy as that.

Also, being "the nice guy" who does free work doesn't get you very far. If you keep throwing in extra tasks without proper documentation, homeowners will start to take it for granted. They won't value your work, and worse, they might still be unsatisfied, expecting more. You could end up having to redo work that was never agreed upon in the first place. So protect yourself—use change orders and get paid up front before the work is done.

MANAGING SUBS

Managing subcontractors can feel like juggling, especially when homeowners think they can bypass you and deal with your subs directly. I have an entire bonus chapter dedicated to managing subs, but it is important to highlight an important pitfall when it comes to change orders.

Oftentimes, a homeowner will request additional work from a subcontractor without your knowledge. The sub, wanting to please, does the work without a change order, and suddenly, you're stuck with an unexpected bill. That's a problem, and it can escalate quickly if you're not careful.

This is why it's so important to include clear terms in your contract about who has the authority to approve extra work. Spell it out: Homeowners must direct all change order requests to the project manager—not the subcontractors. For example, your contract might say, "Only the project manager is authorized to approve additional work or changes to the scope of the project. Subcontractors are not permitted to accept or act on requests from homeowners directly." By laying down this rule, you avoid miscommunication and ensure that you stay in control of the process.

Set expectations early. When you're having that conversation with your client before the project even starts, make it clear: "If you want to change anything or add extra work, talk to me, not my crew." That way, you maintain control, ensure proper documentation, and avoid confusion down the road.

But the responsibility doesn't stop there. You need to manage your subs, too. Let them know that if a homeowner approaches them with requests, they are to direct that homeowner right back to you. Subs should never make promises or start extra work without your approval, and it's your job to enforce that rule. This extra communication, though it might seem small, can save you major headaches later.

In short, keep communication tight. Manage your subs, educate your clients, and document everything. Doing so will protect your business, your project, and your sanity in the long run.

THE ASPIRING BUILDER

Ted was excited. He had experience building houses—just never for anyone other than himself. This project was a big deal: his first real client. A homeowner hired Ted to build a brand-new home from the ground up, and Ted couldn't wait to prove himself. But this wasn't just any homeowner. Unbeknownst to Ted, this client had done his homework, and it wasn't the kind of research you'd expect.

The homeowner had tracked down what properties Ted owned and made sure to include a personal guarantee in the contract. Now, if Ted didn't fulfill his end of the deal, the homeowner wouldn't just go after the business—Ted's personal assets were on the line. But Ted, eager to get the job done, didn't give it much thought.

From day one, the job seemed simple enough. Ted had a contract, a clear scope of work, and a set of blueprints. The project started smoothly, but as it progressed, the homeowner began requesting changes. Small things at first—minor adjustments to the plans. Ted, wanting to keep the client happy, went ahead and made the changes. *No problem*, he thought. *I'll get a change order for this later.* That became the refrain throughout the build. The homeowner would say, "Just take care of this now, and we'll sort out the paperwork at the end."

Ted, eager to please and avoid conflict, kept obliging. As the months passed, those small changes accumulated. By the time the house was 90 percent finished, Ted realized he was looking at $150,000 worth of additional work—none of which had been properly documented with a signed change order.

When Ted approached the homeowner to collect for the extra work, everything came crashing down. Instead of agreeing to pay, the homeowner outright refused and terminated Ted from the job. Ted was stunned. How could someone back out after all the work had been done? His frustration mounted when the homeowner not only refused to pay, but also sued Ted for not finishing the project and for defective work.

Ted's $150,000 dream project was now a legal nightmare.

He had no signed change orders to back him up, and his personal assets were now on the line because of the personal guarantee he had signed. The case became even more complicated when Ted discovered the homeowner had been planning this all along. The entire setup was designed for Ted to fail, allowing the homeowner to come after his assets.

In a last-ditch effort, Ted filed a lien for the unpaid work. The homeowner countered by suing Ted, claiming the work was incomplete and defective. The case dragged on, with both sides trading legal blows. But then, something unexpected happened.

When Ted's team went to court to argue the validity of the lien, the judge sided with Ted. The judgment declared the lien valid and included a finality clause, meaning that the case was closed (more on lien rights in Chapter 7). Because of that language, Ted's client couldn't pursue the lawsuit further. It was an unusual outcome, and one that didn't typically happen in such cases. While Ted didn't recover everything he was owed, he managed to avoid paying the homeowner anything in return.

Ted's first client project had taken a turn he never saw coming. He walked away bruised but with his assets intact—a hard lesson learned about the value of change orders and proper documentation.

EXAMPLE CONTRACT LANGUAGE

To make sure you're covered, here is an example of what your contract should include:

> "The Owner may request changes to the Work. All changes must be documented in a written Change Order signed by both parties. The cost of extra Work will be added to the Contract Price, and payments for extra Work will be made as it progresses alongside regular payments.
>
> **Important:** No additional Work will begin without a signed Change Order.
>
> 1. **For Increases in Work**
>   a. A signed Change Order must describe the additional Work, cost, and any required extension of the completion date.
>   b. If extra Work requires additional time, the Contractor is entitled to a reasonable extension.
>
> 3. **For Decreases in Work**
>   d. The Owner and Contractor must agree on the reduced scope and Contract Price.
>   e. If no agreement is reached, the reduction will equal the cost of materials plus 15 percent.
>
> Amendments signed or initialed by both parties will become part of the Contract and control over conflicting terms."

> **KEY TAKEAWAYS**
>
> - Set expectations early about the change order process. This will make you look like the expert that you are.
> - You are not entitled to get paid for extra work that isn't documented. Don't do it!
> - Consider charging a fee for change orders as leverage.

AN IMPORTANT LIFELINE

In the unpredictable world of construction, change orders are your lifeline to maintaining order, transparency, and profitability. Ted learned this lesson the hard way. By failing to document every change with a signed order, he nearly lost everything. His eagerness to please and avoid conflict left him vulnerable to a client who had other plans. Ted's story is a powerful reminder that without a clear change order process, you risk losing time, money, and trust.

Remember, every change—big or small—needs to be documented in writing and agreed upon before any work begins. By educating your clients, managing your subcontractors, and being diligent with paperwork, you create a framework that minimizes disputes and maximizes success.

But let's face it: Sometimes, no matter how clearly you set expectations, some projects can turn into a colossal nightmare. Whether it's because of an uncooperative client, unforeseen complications, or changing circumstances, there may come a time when you need to walk away—but you won't be able to do that without an escape clause, which we'll cover in the next chapter.

CHAPTER 6

ESCAPE CLAUSE

Construction is just like marriage.

Wait, what?

That's right—think about it! Both start with big dreams, a lot of excitement, and the promise to build something beautiful together. But, just like in marriage, there are times when things don't go as planned.

Maybe the homeowner turns into a bridezilla, or unforeseen circumstances make you want to run for the hills. So, what do you do? You protect yourself with a prenup—or if you're in construction, an escape clause!

An escape clause in a construction contract is like a prenup for builders. It's not about predicting disaster—it's about being smart. If things go south, this clause gives both parties a way to call it quits without dragging each other through a messy divorce. You get paid for the work you've done, the homeowner finds someone else to finish their "dream house," and everyone walks away with their dignity and wallets intact.

In this chapter, we'll explore the essential role of the escape clause in construction contracts—your built-in safety net that allows for a clean exit when things go awry. You'll learn how this provision protects both contractors and homeowners from unexpected challenges, minimizes financial risk, and ensures a fair resolution if a project doesn't go as planned.

WHAT IS AN ESCAPE CLAUSE?

An escape clause allows you to walk away from a contract without breaching it, essentially giving you a legal exit. It allows you to cancel your contract with forty-eight hours' notice, regardless of the reason. You'll be paid for the work you've done up to that point, and you'll refund any money you haven't spent.

Here is an example of the language you should include in your contract: *"Contractor can cancel the contract for any reason or no reason at all with forty-eight hours' notice."*

It's simple, right? Yes, but only if you include an escape clause in your contract. If you don't, walking away without proper notice or reason means breaching the contract, and that opens you up to financial consequences.

And I'm talking about serious numbers here.

Let's say you're remodeling a kitchen, and your contract quotes $100,000 for the job. Halfway through, you and the homeowner are at each other's throats. The tension is too much, and you walk off the job. The homeowner hires someone else to finish the work, but the new contractor charges $130,000 for the same scope. Guess who's liable for that extra $30,000?

You are.

Walking away doesn't just mean forfeiting what you're owed—it can mean paying out of pocket for someone else to finish the job—and that's why an escape clause is so important. It allows you to exit a contract without being in breach, protecting you from legal and financial headaches.

WHY YOU NEED THIS CLAUSE

We've already covered that contracts are promises—solid, legal promises. You're agreeing to complete a certain scope of work for a certain amount of money. When you sign that contract, you're bound by its terms. But what happens when life throws a wrench in your plans? What if the homeowner becomes impossible to deal with? What if there's a personal emergency, or supply chain issues delay your project indefinitely?

Without an escape clause, none of these situations are valid reasons to cancel the contract. You're still on the hook to finish the work, even if you don't want to or can't. Reasons like toxic clients, family emergencies, illness, or material shortages *do not* release you from your contractual obligations. Unless you've built in the escape clause, you're stuck, no matter how justified you feel in wanting to leave.

But even with the clause, it's important to understand how to use it properly. You can't just up and leave without notice. The escape clause typically requires that you give the homeowner a heads-up—usually forty-eight hours—before terminating the contract. Once you've given notice, you're free to exit, refund any unused funds, and get paid for the work completed without worrying about legal repercussions.

The escape clause is one of the most important sections of any contract. Without it, you could be tethered to a project that's not worth your time, energy, or health. So, make sure it's in every contract you sign. Not having an escape clause could mean opening yourself up to damages, lawsuits, and financial losses that are completely avoidable.

By including this clause, you're giving yourself the flexibility to walk away from a project without breaching your agreement. And sometimes, that flexibility can extend to renegotiating the terms of your contract after misquoting a project, as we will see in Kevin's story.

UNDERBIDDING A PROJECT

Kevin had been in the construction business for a while. He took on a project in Michigan, bidding on a job that seemed straightforward enough. Everything looked good on paper—until he realized he'd severely underbid. He'd forgotten to include $20,000 worth of work in his pricing. Now, if he finished the project as promised, he'd be paying out of his own pocket.

Suddenly, the project wasn't just about getting the job done—it was about saving his business from a financial blow.

The missing $20,000 wasn't just a minor oversight. It was a significant chunk of the project's budget, and Kevin faced a tough decision. He could walk away and risk being sued, leaving himself on the hook for any additional costs the homeowner would incur to finish the project. Or he could finish the job, absorb the $20,000 loss, and move on, knowing it would be a painful but invaluable lesson.

Kevin chose the latter, deciding to eat the cost and finish the work. It was a hard pill to swallow, but it saved him from a lawsuit and more financial damage down the road. He walked away with a bruised ego and a lighter wallet, but his business survived.

Now, if Kevin had included an escape clause in his contract, the story might have played out differently. Instead of eating the $20,000 loss, he could have gone back to the homeowner and said, "Look, I underbid this project. I can't finish it unless we renegotiate the terms. Here's our options: Either we add this amount to the contract, or I'll have to cancel."

An escape clause wouldn't have just let Kevin walk away. It would have opened the door to a renegotiation, giving the homeowner a choice: Either adjust the contract to include the missed costs, or find someone else to finish the job. This would have been a clean way out, legally protected, and could have even led to a fair compromise.

Had Kevin used the escape clause, the homeowner might have been upset—no one likes hearing they'll have to pay more—but that's part of the negotiation. The homeowner might have explored other options, such as getting new bids to see if another contractor could finish the job for less. In many cases, however, homeowners opt to continue with the original contractor if the relationship is still intact and the price adjustment is reasonable.

Kevin could have ended up with a change order in place, adding the $20,000 to the contract, and continued the project without the financial hit. It would have been a far less painful way to handle the situation.

Even without an escape clause, it's important to remember that you can always talk to the homeowner. You never know what they'll say. In Kevin's case, he chose to eat the cost, but a conversation might have opened up the possibility of splitting it. Many homeowners appreciate the honesty, and I've often witnessed they're willing to meet the contractor halfway. After all, no homeowner wants the contractor cutting corners elsewhere to make up for lost money.

Kevin's situation teaches a valuable lesson: Mistakes happen, and sometimes they're costly. But with an escape clause in your contract, you give yourself the flexibility to renegotiate when things go sideways.

YOU'RE IN BREACH: NOW WHAT?

If you decided to walk away from a job for whatever reason, what would happen?

Well, the first thing to happen comes in the form of a demand letter.

A demand letter is usually the first step in the legal process. It's like an official warning, often from an attorney, saying, "Hey, you didn't follow through with the contract, and my client has been damaged as a result." This letter will outline the alleged breach and the financial damages the homeowner claims you're responsible for. The demand could be something like, "Come back and finish the work" or, "We're hiring someone else, and you'll be liable for the extra costs."

In some states, especially with residential construction contracts, homeowners are required to send you a demand letter before they can even think about filing a lawsuit. It's your opportunity to fix things before things escalate to court.

The most important thing to do if you receive a demand letter is *not* to ignore it. Here are four steps to follow if you receive one:

STEP ONE: DON'T PANIC

Receiving a demand letter can be intimidating, but the first thing you need to do is stay calm. As long as you respond within the given timeframe—usually thirty to sixty days—you're still in control. Panicking won't help; planning will.

STEP TWO: GATHER YOUR DOCUMENTS

This is where preparation is key. As soon as you receive that demand letter, you need to collect everything: contracts, change orders, emails, text messages, photos—any documentation related to the project. The more you have, the better you'll be able to defend yourself. Memories fade, so it's also a good idea to create a detailed timeline of events, jotting down everything you remember about the project. This will help you keep your facts straight as the case moves forward.

STEP THREE: CALL YOUR ATTORNEY

Once you've gathered your documents and made a timeline, it's time to get your attorney involved. Show them the demand letter and all your supporting evidence. Your lawyer will usually draft a response letter, sometimes with a settlement offer or a proposal to finish the work. The goal is to resolve the issue quickly before it spirals into a full-blown lawsuit.

Here's the good news: In about 95 percent of cases, if you address the demand letter at this stage, the issue can be settled out of court. Most homeowners just want the work completed, and by engaging early, you might be able to finish the job or negotiate a reasonable settlement.

WHAT HAPPENS IF YOU IGNORE THE DEMAND LETTER?

Now, what if you ignore the demand letter? This is where things get costly—fast. After thirty or sixty days of no response, the homeowner will likely file a lawsuit. When that happens, you'll not only be defending the breach of contract claim, but you'll also have to deal with the fact that they had to hire an attorney, and guess what? You could be responsible for their legal fees too.

By the time you reach the lawsuit stage, you're already playing catch-up. The chances of settling for a reasonable amount are much slimmer, and the costs skyrocket. What might have been settled for a few thousand dollars in the demand letter stage could now balloon into hundreds of thousands of dollars in legal fees, damages, and other penalties.

Ignoring the demand letter and letting the case progress to court can be disastrous. If you go to trial and lose, you could be on the hook for the homeowner's damages, attorney's fees, and potentially your own legal costs. And if you didn't include an escape clause in your contract, there's no easy way out—you're fully liable.

In short, you could go from paying a small settlement during the demand letter phase to owing hundreds of thousands of dollars after a drawn-out lawsuit.

I cannot stress this enough: Do not ignore the demand letter!

The demand letter is the first domino in what could become a very expensive and time-consuming litigation process. But here's the silver lining: As long as you don't ignore it, you have options. You could settle, finish the work, or negotiate a deal. But the moment you ignore it, you lose control.

By responding promptly and preparing a strong case with all your documents in order, you can often resolve the issue without ever seeing the inside of a courtroom. And that's the best outcome anyone can hope for in these situations.

THE POWER OF AN ESCAPE CLAUSE IN COURT

Let's say you've been smart. You included an escape clause in your contract. Now, despite that, the homeowner sues you. What happens next? Well, that escape clause might just be your saving grace.

When you've got an escape clause, your chances of quickly getting out of a legal mess increase dramatically. Once the lawsuit is filed, your attorney can submit a motion to the court, essentially saying, "Hey, judge, my client didn't do anything wrong here. Their contract allows them to leave the project, no questions asked." With that, you could be out of court much faster, sidestepping drawn-out legal battles.

The escape clause clearly states that you have the right to cancel or walk away from the project, with proper notice, without breaching the contract. So, when the homeowner tries to claim otherwise, the clause acts as a solid defense. In most cases, this is enough to stop the lawsuit dead in its tracks.

When the homeowner's attorney receives a response from your side, outlining that you had every legal right to leave because of the escape clause, the case often ends right there. Any competent attorney will take a look at your contract, see the escape clause, and realize that pursuing the case won't go far. They'll likely advise their client to drop the lawsuit rather than waste time and money on a losing battle.

Sure, there are some attorneys who may push forward—not necessarily because it's in their client's best interest, but because they're trying to bill more hours. It happens.

But even in those rare cases, the escape clause remains your shield. In most instances, the case fizzles out as soon as the clause is brought to light.

Having an escape clause isn't just about avoiding lawsuits; it's about doing so quickly and efficiently. Without one, you're forced to navigate the full legal process, which can be slow, expensive, and stressful. But with an escape clause in place, you can file a motion that says, "I followed the terms of the contract, I'm not in breach, and I'm out." It's as close to a legal parachute as you can get.

> **KEY TAKEAWAYS**
>
> - Leave yourself a way out with an escape clause, otherwise you could be in breach of contract.
> - You could be liable for damages without an escape clause.
> - The escape clause gives you the opportunity to walk away from the contract without being in breach.

A CLEAN BREAK

Just like a prenup, an escape clause sets you up for a clean break. No drama, no lawsuits, no awkward alimony payments—just a mutual agreement that says, "Hey, this isn't working out."

An escape clause isn't just a safety net; it's a smart strategy for protecting your business when the unexpected happens. As we've seen with Kevin's story, having this clause could have saved him from a costly mistake that nearly put him out of business. By providing a clear path to exit a project when necessary, an escape clause minimizes financial risk, prevents legal headaches, and preserves your peace of mind.

Without an escape clause, you're left vulnerable to situations that could drain your time, money, and sanity. Including this provision in every contract gives you the flexibility to handle unforeseen challenges and ensure both you and your client have a fair way out if things go south.

Before signing any contract, you better include payment terms—and discuss them with your clients. We cover what that looks like next.

CHAPTER 7
———

PAYMENT TERMS

If you're not clear about when you expect to be paid, guess what? You probably won't get paid!

Cash flow is the lifeblood of your business—without it, everything grinds to a halt. That's why having a clear, perfected billing process isn't just a nice-to-have; it's essential. This means setting up a system that ensures you get paid on time, every time, so you can keep your projects moving forward, pay your team, and cover your expenses. But it all starts with having the right language in your contract.

Your contract is where you lay out exactly how and when you expect to be paid, what happens if payments are delayed, and how you'll handle nonpayment. It's not just about listing numbers on a page; it's about setting clear expectations with your clients and giving yourself the legal footing to take action if things go wrong.

Being in construction, you're going to run into situations where clients drag their feet or flat-out refuse to pay. It's just part of the game. That's why your contract needs to include a solid plan for handling nonpayment and collections. This could mean charging late fees, stopping work until the issue is resolved, or even terminating the contract if payments fall too far behind.

Without a perfected billing process outlined in your contract, you're left scrambling, hoping clients will do the right thing. But hope isn't a business strategy. With a clear, well-drafted billing process, you set the rules upfront, minimize misunderstandings, and ensure you have the cash to keep your business running smoothly.

In this chapter, we'll explore what to do when a homeowner fails to pay. From sending demand letters to knowing when to stop work, you'll learn how to protect your business with a clear, consistent collection strategy. We'll also cover why it's essential to understand your lien rights, plan for insurance-related nonpayments, and make sure your contract gives you the leverage to get paid on time.

SETTING PAYMENT TERMS

At the most basic level, payment terms define when and how you get paid. Some contractors prefer to set up payments based on milestones (e.g., "once the cabinets are installed, this amount is due"), while others bill based on percentages of completion. For residential projects, it's often a good idea to bill in advance before starting a new phase, but be fair—don't get too far ahead of the work. For example, once you're ready to start the granite countertops, make sure you're paid for that stage before lifting a finger. Whether you choose to use percentages or milestones, just be clear about it in the contract.

It's easy for contractors to see when a milestone has been reached, but that might not be obvious to a homeowner. So, make it clear: Send an invoice as soon as you hit a payment point. "Hey, we've completed this milestone, and the next payment is due." And don't just hope the homeowner will pay on time. Include in your contract that payments must be received within a set period—I suggest three to five business days.

If the homeowner drags their feet on payment, you need to protect yourself. Your contract should clearly state that if payment isn't received within the specified time, you have the right to stop working. And it's not just about halting the project; you can also stipulate that once work stops, the project schedule will shift. This means if you have other clients lined up, they'll take priority, and the homeowner's project gets bumped until you have an opening again. Additionally, if payment is more than sixty days overdue, your contract should give you the right to cancel the agreement altogether. Having these clauses in place gives you leverage. You can say, "I haven't received payment, so I'm stopping work until this is resolved," and you'll have the contract to back you up.

Payment terms are one of the most critical parts of the contract, and you should go over them with every homeowner. This is about setting expectations from the get-go. Explain how the payment schedule works and what happens if payments are late, and make it clear that you will stop work or cancel the project if payment isn't made on time. Clear terms aren't just for your benefit; they help clients understand exactly what to expect and can prevent misunderstandings.

Be aware that some states have specific laws about how much of a deposit you can take. For example, in California, the limit is the smaller of 10 percent of the total contract price or $1,000. Not many states have strict limits, but it's essential to check your local regulations and ensure you're in compliance.

One of the biggest mistakes contractors make is doing extra work without getting paid for it, all because they want to be nice. Here's the thing—being a "nice guy" doesn't mean running your business into the ground. Be a nice guy to yourself first. Stick to your contract, don't start new phases without payment, and don't get roped into doing freebies. Your contract is there to protect you, and it'll make your life (and your business) a lot smoother if you use it. So set your terms, explain them clearly, and follow them.

A NOTE ON CREDIT CARD PAYMENTS

Accepting payments via credit card can be convenient but also fraught with potential pitfalls. One common issue we face is credit card fraud. For example, imagine a scenario where you complete a substantial amount of work and accept a credit card payment. However, shortly after, the customer disputes the charge, claiming that the transaction was fraudulent.

In such cases, the credit card company may temporarily withdraw the funds from your account while they investigate the dispute. This investigation can be particularly challenging if you do not have strong proof of the transaction's legitimacy.

To mitigate these risks, it's crucial to obtain a credit card authorization for each payment. This helps establish that the payment was legitimate and authorized. If the dispute progresses, having clear records of the authorization can be vital in proving that you are entitled to the money. Credit card companies like American Express tend to favor their customers during disputes, but having robust records increases the likelihood of a favorable resolution for you.

While credit card payments can be useful, contractors should be vigilant and maintain thorough documentation to protect themselves against potential disputes and fraud.

LIEN RIGHTS: PROTECTING WHAT YOU'RE OWED

Knowing your lien rights is essential for protecting the money you're owed. These rights, which date back to the founding of the United States, are among the oldest laws on the books. In fact, they originated with Thomas Jefferson, who needed to reassure construction workers (then known as "mechanics") that they would get paid for building the Capitol. At the time, the US was a new nation, and contractors were hesitant to work without some form of security. Jefferson promised that if they didn't get paid, they could place a lien on the property, giving them a legal right to be compensated. This concept has stuck around for centuries, and today, every state has its own version of these protections.

As a contractor, your lien rights give you a secure debt rather than an unsecured one. If you only have a breach of contract claim, it's like trying to collect credit card debt—you'd have to sue, win, and then find assets to collect from. But with a lien, it's a whole different ball game. Your debt is secured by the property you improved, meaning if you're not paid, you can force the sale of the property (just like a mortgage) to satisfy the amount owed. This leverage can make a huge difference in getting paid because the homeowner can't sell, refinance, or get permanent financing until the lien is resolved.

In most states, if you provide labor or materials that improve a property's value, you have the right to file a mechanics and materials lien for the value you added. But to use this right, you need to follow specific rules. Each state has its own requirements—like sending certain notices within a set timeframe and filing the lien properly. Some states even mandate that your contract must mention your right to file a lien if you're not paid. For example, in California, if you're not working directly with the homeowner, you need to send notice to the owner within twenty days of starting work.

Understanding these requirements and building them into your collection strategy is crucial. Most of the time, residential projects don't escalate to lien filings—it's more common on the commercial side. However, knowing your rights can be a powerful tool if you're dealing with a nonpaying client. If you don't protect your lien rights, you could miss the window to file, leaving you without a way to recover the money you're owed. Worse yet, in some states, if you don't have a written contract, you might not have lien rights at all. About 75 percent of states have licensing requirements tied to lien rights, so failing to comply could mean losing out on payment altogether.

I've studied lien laws across all fifty states, and they vary widely. Everything from when you need to send notice, to when a lien must be filed, to how long the lien remains valid is different depending on where you're working. That's why it's essential to know the rules for your state and make sure you're prepared to act if a client doesn't pay.

Having a solid collection strategy is key to keeping your cash flow healthy. This means setting up milestone payments, issuing invoices promptly, and giving yourself the right to stop work if payments aren't made. But what happens if you've done all that and still aren't getting paid? That's where your lien rights come in. They're the next step in your collection process and a crucial part of making sure your business stays afloat, especially when you're staring down a year-end balance sheet and trying to keep the books in order.

The worst situation is having a collection issue without a plan in place. Missing your lien rights can mean being left with no way to recover what you're owed. So, understand the rules, build a strategy, and don't let a nonpaying client ruin your business.

THE POOL CONTRACTOR'S NIGHTMARE

Let me tell you about Maurice, a pool contractor who thought he had landed his dream project. A client had hired him to build a massive, custom pool with all the bells and whistles—waterfalls, a swim-up bar, and even a lazy river that wrapped around the backyard. It was a serious job, but Maurice was excited. This was going to be one of those projects that could really put his company on the map. He could already imagine the photos he'd be snapping for his website, showing off this backyard paradise.

The client, let's call her "Karen," seemed thrilled at first. She was giddy as Maurice's team got to work, pouring concrete, shaping the lazy river, and transforming her yard into a mini waterpark. And the best part? They were moving fast. Within about thirty to fifty days, they'd made serious progress—most of the concrete was down, the pool structure was complete, and they were just starting to install the finishing touches.

But then, just as things were coming together, Karen

pulled a 180. Out of nowhere, she decided that Maurice's team was charging too much. She started nitpicking every detail, from the color of the concrete to the angle of the water jets. Maurice could sense trouble brewing, but he figured they could smooth things over. After all, he had a solid contract, and the work was almost done.

That's when Karen dropped the bomb: She canceled all of her payments. Every single one. She called up her credit card company and disputed the charges, claiming that the work was unsatisfactory and that she shouldn't have to pay for it. Maurice's jaw hit the floor. He couldn't believe it—his team had been busting their butts, working late, and pushing through the summer heat to make sure everything was perfect. They'd done the work, they had the receipts to prove it, but now the payments were just...gone.

Maurice thought the credit card company would see reason. Surely, they'd take one look at his contract, see that the work had been completed, and restore the funds. But that's not what happened. The credit card company sided with Karen, and just like that, Maurice was out thousands of dollars. He couldn't get back the money he was owed, even though he had done everything by the book.

Desperate and unsure of what to do next, Maurice called

me to see if there was anything that could be done. That's when I explained the lien process to him. It was serious leverage, and in Maurice's case, it was his best shot at getting his money back.

We filed a mechanics lien on Karen's property, which legally prevented her from selling or refinancing until the lien was resolved.

Karen's pool paradise had now become her problem. With the lien filed, she couldn't escape the reality of what she owed. She'd either have to pay Maurice what she originally agreed to, or deal with the legal mess of a lien on her property. When Karen realized she wasn't getting away scot-free, she quickly changed her tune. After a tense round of negotiations, she finally agreed to settle up with Maurice, and the funds were transferred directly to his account.

YOU ARE OWED MONEY, NOW WHAT?

When a homeowner isn't paying up, you've got a few options. The first step is often sending a demand letter. This is a formal way of saying, "Hey, you owe me money. Let's settle this before things get ugly." Ideally, the homeowner responds, and you can work out a payment or reach an agreement. But if they don't, then you have to consider taking more serious action, like filing a lawsuit.

Before jumping straight into a lawsuit, though, you need to assess the situation carefully. Consider your relationship with the homeowner and the potential risks. Are they likely to countersue and start nitpicking everything they're unhappy with, real or imagined? Sometimes, filing a suit might lead to a bigger headache than it's worth, especially if you end up paying legal fees or losing more than you stood to gain. This isn't to say you should never sue—just be smart about it. If you're talking about $20,000 or more, sending a demand letter and having a few firm phone calls might push things in the right direction.

If those efforts still don't work and the homeowner doesn't respond, you'll have to decide whether to proceed with a lawsuit. But before it gets to that point, there's one crucial strategy: Stop working as soon as payment issues arise. If a client is hesitant to pay or keeps putting off payments, you shouldn't keep working and hope they'll catch up later. They probably won't. Respect your time and effort—stop working and invoke the terms of your contract. This will keep you in a much better position.

If you stop work when payments dry up, you're less likely to end up in a big, messy fight. Continuing to work without payment often leads to disputes that become far more personal and emotional than you anticipated. Suddenly, every little thing they didn't like comes out, and what was a simple payment issue turns into a much bigger battle.

INSURANCE-RELATED NONPAYMENT

Some of the biggest nonpayment issues happen when homeowners receive insurance payouts for damage repair, but then don't pass the money along to the contractor. Here's how it typically goes: The homeowner files a claim for something like roof damage, the insurance company issues a check to the homeowner, and the homeowner is supposed to use that money to pay the contractor. But sometimes, homeowners see that check and think, "Wow, I've never had this much money in my hands before. Maybe I'll just hang onto it."

This is especially common in damage and repair work. The insurance company pays the homeowner directly, not the contractor, so if the homeowner decides to keep the money, the contractor is left unpaid. In these situations, you might have to sue, but even then, collecting the money can be tricky. For example, in states like Texas, a person's home is protected from being taken to pay off debts, so even if you win a lawsuit, you might struggle to collect anything.

The key to avoiding these situations is having a consistent collection strategy. Your contract should make it clear that if you're not paid, you have the right to stop work immediately. This needs to be enforced every time there's a payment delay. Don't let the homeowner string you along with promises of a lump sum at the end of the project. Sticking to this policy protects your cash flow and prevents you from getting too deep into a project without seeing any money.

This is particularly important if you're a small business running things on a tight budget. You need leverage to ensure your work is compensated promptly. That means setting up clear payment schedules, sending invoices as soon as milestones are reached, and stopping work if the cash isn't coming in.

Understanding your cash flow and planning around it is essential for any contractor. If you're running a smaller operation, you're likely operating on tight margins. You can't afford to have large amounts of unpaid work hanging over your head, so you need to know exactly when payments are due, what to do if they're late, and how to keep your cash flow steady. Make sure your contract gives you the right to pause work and a plan for what to do next, whether that's sending demand letters, filing liens, or moving toward a lawsuit.

The worst situation is finding yourself owed a ton of money without a plan to recover it. Did you miss your lien rights? Are you left empty-handed because the homeowner is hiding behind legal loopholes? If you don't have a solid strategy, you could end up with no way to get paid. Your best bet is to have everything in writing, understand the rules, and be prepared to take action when needed.

> **KEY TAKEAWAYS**
>
> - Have up front payment scheduled.
> - Don't forget to send invoices!
> - Homeowners need to know when payments are due.
> - Know what your lien rights are to protect the amount that you're owed (secured debt, a lot of leverage). Lien rights are as old as the country and were created to protect the people who work and improve property.

KEEP YOUR BUSINESS RUNNING SMOOTHLY

Nonpayment is one of the biggest challenges contractors face, but with the right approach, you can minimize the risk and protect your business. Having a solid plan in place—one that includes clear payment terms, a consistent collection strategy, and an understanding of your lien rights—will help you handle issues before they spiral out of control. Always stop work when payments are delayed, and don't rely on vague promises or goodwill to see you through. By taking these steps, you'll maintain your cash flow, keep your business running smoothly, and avoid the headaches that come with chasing down money you're owed.

In the next chapter, we'll cover how to communicate project timelines effectively, helping you set clear expectations and keep your clients on track from start to finish.

CHAPTER 8

PROJECT SCHEDULE

Finish early, you are a hero. Finish late, you are a zero.

Let me tell you about Randy, a contractor who learned the hard way why setting a realistic completion date is crucial. He was hired by the Sanders family to build a custom home, and everyone was excited to get started. The Sanderses had big plans—they'd picked out the perfect lot, envisioned a smooth move-in over the summer, and were planning to switch their kids from private to public school in the fall once they were settled. Everything hinged on the home being completed on time, and Randy assured them it would be ready.

But as often happens, things didn't go according to plan. Randy had given them an ambitious completion date, one that didn't account for potential delays. Sure enough, the project hit a few bumps, including unexpected supply issues and a freezing cold snap in Texas that halted work for days. By the time summer rolled around, the house was far from finished.

The Sanderses were left scrambling. They had only signed a lease on a temporary apartment until the date they'd been promised, so they had to extend it—and pay for the extra months out of pocket. Since the house wasn't ready, they couldn't move in, which meant they had to keep their kids in private school for another semester instead of switching to public, adding even more unexpected costs. On top of all that, they continued to pay the mortgage on a home they weren't living in yet.

As you can imagine, they were furious.

When the project was finally done, the Sanderses weren't just ready to move in; they were ready to take Randy to court. They filed a lawsuit, demanding compensation for all the extra costs they had incurred—extra rent, additional private school tuition, and interest on their mortgage.

Since Randy didn't finish on time, they argued they should be reimbursed for the financial fallout.

In the end, they managed to reach a settlement. Randy

had to pay out some compensation, but not nearly as much as the Sanderses were demanding. Still, it was a tough pill to swallow. Randy realized that by giving an overly optimistic completion date, he had set himself up for failure from the start. The Sanderses had planned their lives around that promise, and when it wasn't kept, everything unraveled.

In this chapter, you'll learn why setting a completion date is like setting a goal—it needs to be realistic, be flexible, and account for the unexpected. We'll cover how to build in buffers, communicate that the completion date is a target rather than a guarantee, and avoid making promises that could lead to costly legal battles, damaged reputations, and unhappy clients.

PROJECT SCHEDULES

While the payment terms we covered in the last chapter may be the most important part of the contract for you, the schedule is the most important to the homeowner.

Managing project schedules can sometimes feel like navigating a ship through stormy seas. Delays are a part of the job, but how you handle them can make or break your business.

In Randy's case, a rare Texas freeze caused pipes to burst

and flood a house under renovation. The Sanders family, displaced and crammed into a small apartment, anxiously counted down the days until they could finally move into their new home. But when Randy's project timeline stretched beyond what he had promised, the situation quickly escalated. What started as a delay turned into a full-blown legal battle, with the Sanderses suing for all the extra costs they had to cover while waiting for their house to be completed.

And that is why setting realistic completion dates is crucial.

Setting a completion date is akin to setting a goal. It's important, but it needs to be realistic. Perhaps more importantly, a completion date should be a target, not a guarantee. Ensure that it's attainable or include provisions for adjustments, such as extensions for delays caused by weather, material shortages, or unforeseen issues. Otherwise, you risk a breach of contract claim that could cost you dearly.

Setting expectations is key to avoiding disputes. Start by discussing a realistic timeline with homeowners. Explain that construction is inherently unpredictable and that delays are a common part of the process. Include a section in the contract that outlines how delays will be handled and what steps you'll take to minimize them.

This way, homeowners know what to expect and are less likely to be surprised or frustrated if things don't go exactly as planned.

The following represent some best practices for setting completion dates:

1. **Offer an Estimated Date:** Instead of a hard-and-fast deadline, provide an estimated completion date. Clearly state in the contract that this is an approximation and not a guarantee. This way, if delays occur due to unforeseen issues, you won't be held liable for a breach of contract. Make it clear that while you will make every effort to meet this date, it's not a firm deadline, and missing it does not constitute a breach of contract. This way, if delays occur, you're not held liable as long as you're actively working toward the completion.
2. **Utilize Change Orders:** When unexpected events, like a flood, throw a wrench into your schedule, use a change order to adjust the timeline. This document should detail the reasons for the delay and outline a new completion date. This helps protect you from claims of breach of contract. Make sure all change orders are well-documented, ideally with the homeowner's signature. But if getting a signature isn't possible (especially if clients are upset or uncooperative), even a text message or email confirming

the change order can be sufficient. The key is having proof that changes were communicated and acknowledged.
3. **Build in Buffer Time:** Construction projects are rarely straightforward. If you estimate a job will take two months, consider quoting four months. This buffer helps you handle unexpected issues without blowing the deadline and makes you look like a hero if you finish early.

SELECTIONS AND DEADLINES

Another key factor in keeping your project on schedule is making sure the homeowner sticks to deadlines for selections, like choosing materials, finishes, or fixtures. Your contract should clearly state that the project timeline depends on clients making timely decisions. For example, you might write that the homeowner has two weeks to make their selections. If they take longer than that, extra days will be added to the project completion date.

Some contractors go a step further and include a clause that imposes a fee for delays—such as charging $100 for every week the homeowner fails to make their selections within the specified timeframe. While this approach can be hit or miss, it helps emphasize that keeping to the schedule is a two-way street. Yes, you'll do your part to meet deadlines, but the homeowner needs to do theirs as well. If they drag their feet on making decisions, it's only fair that the timeline gets extended, and they may even incur extra costs.

This is why it's so important to have a conversation about the schedule and expectations up front. Homeowners need to understand that it's not just a matter of signing the contract and stepping back. They have to be engaged throughout the process. When you ask them to make decisions, they need to respond promptly. If they don't, it's going to hold up the project—and they can't expect the original timeline to be met when they're the ones causing delays.

Including a fine for delays can be a good way to encourage respect for the timeline and everyone's time. It sends a clear message: Don't waste the time of the project or the people working on it. And even if you have this clause, you're not obligated to enforce it. Think of it like a cancellation fee; it gives you the option to charge for delays if you choose to, but it's mainly there as a tool to keep things moving. This way, homeowners are more likely to understand how important it is for them to make timely selections, and it ensures that everyone is on the same page about what needs to happen to keep the project on track.

PRO TIPS FOR KEEPING YOUR PROJECTS (AND SANITY) ON TRACK

Here I go again: Success often comes down to managing expectations, handling changes, and keeping communication clear. Here are some key strategies to help you navigate projects more smoothly:

1. **Under-Promise and Over-Deliver:** Always aim to exceed expectations rather than just meet them. Set realistic timelines that allow for a buffer, so if you finish early, homeowners will be thrilled and sing your praises. On the flip side, if you finish late, you risk a disappointed client and the possibility of a negative review—or worse, a legal dispute. Setting realistic goals from the outset can make all the difference.
2. **Align Milestone Payments with Project Phases:** Coordinate milestone payments with specific phases of the project. This helps maintain your cash flow and provides a clear framework for both you and the homeowner. When payments are tied to tangible progress, it's easier to keep clients informed and manage expectations.
3. **Communicate Clearly and Regularly:** Regular updates are essential for keeping homeowners informed and avoiding surprises. Consistent communication about project progress, potential delays, and any issues that might affect the timeline builds trust and minimizes the risk of disputes. Always document

these updates, whether via email or formal notices, so you have a record if disagreements arise.
4. **Include a Non-Consequential Damages Clause:** To protect yourself from being liable for indirect costs that might arise due to delays—like extra rent, storage fees, or other consequential damages—make sure your contract includes a non-consequential damages clause. Simply include this sentence in your contract that serves as a catch-all for whatever the homeowner may try to blame you for: "I am not responsible for any consequential damages that may arise from the project." This ensures that if the project timeline overruns, you're not on the hook for expenses beyond the scope of your work (more on this in Chapter 14).

By following these strategies, you can better manage project schedules and reduce the risk of legal disputes. Balancing realistic expectations with clear contractual terms and effective communication will not only keep your clients happy, but also help maintain a smooth, successful operation. Being prepared, transparent, and proactive can turn potential pitfalls into opportunities for building stronger client relationships and a more resilient business.

> **KEY TAKEAWAYS**
>
> - Address what a realistic schedule is before you start the project.
> - Add more time in writing via change orders when needed.
> - Communicate early and often.

HOPE IS NOT A STRATEGY

Managing project schedules is about more than just setting a date and hoping you hit it. You need to build in flexibility, make sure everyone understands what to expect, and be prepared to adjust if things don't go as planned.

Randy's story is a cautionary tale for any contractor who thinks they can set an optimistic completion date and hope for the best. In his case, promising a tight timeline without accounting for possible delays led to frustrated homeowners, legal battles, and financial consequences. The Sanderses had planned their lives around that timeline, and when it wasn't met, they sought damages. If Randy had taken the time to set realistic expectations, build in buffer time, and communicate clearly with the Sanderses from the start, he might have avoided a lot of headaches—not to mention the lawsuit.

By implementing strategies like clear selection deadlines, realistic timelines, and effective communication, you'll set yourself up for smoother projects, happier clients, and a stronger, more resilient business.

The pandemic sure threw a lot of wrenches into our industry, but some of those challenges could have been mitigated if your contract had some language regarding a plan for the unexpected—which we will cover in the next chapter.

CHAPTER 9

PLAN FOR THE UNEXPECTED

It was a perfect fall day in 2019 when Danny, a roofer who had been in the business for a few years, landed a big project. It wasn't just any project—this was a full roof replacement for a sprawling suburban home owned by a man named Joe Mathers. Mr. Mathers was a friendly guy, and everything seemed to be lined up perfectly. The contract was signed and sealed, and Danny felt pretty confident about the job.

But roofing isn't always a straightforward business, and Danny had a packed schedule. By the time he could fit Mr. Mathers's roof into his lineup, it was early 2021, and things had changed. A lot.

For starters, the cost of materials—shingles, plywood, nails—had jumped 30 percent since the contract was signed. On top of that, there was a labor shortage. The pandemic had slowed down work everywhere, and Danny couldn't find enough guys to get the project off the ground. His usual crew was booked or unavailable, and every attempt to hire new workers hit a dead end.

This put Danny in a tight spot. With the price increases and no crew to help him, he realized finishing this job under the original terms wasn't just difficult—it was impossible. After crunching the numbers, Danny came to the conclusion he would be losing money—possibly tens of thousands of dollars—if he went ahead with the job. So he made a decision he thought was best for his business: He walked away.

"I can't do this," Danny told Mr. Mathers. "I'm sorry but I have to walk away from the project."

Mr. Mathers, needing his roof done, hired another contractor and ended up paying $100,000 to get the job finished. Months passed, and Danny moved on, trying to line up work that made more financial sense. But then the call came—Mr. Mathers was suing him for the $50,000 he paid the new contractor to complete the roof Danny had abandoned.

That's when Danny called me, panicked, looking for advice. "I'm getting sued, and I don't know what to do," he said.

"Take a deep breath, Danny," I said. "Do you have a clause in your contract for price increases or delays? Something to protect you from all these changes that happened?"

There was silence on the other end of the line. "No, I don't have that," Danny admitted.

And there it was. Without that crucial provision, there wasn't much I could do. I gave him a few pointers—maybe he could negotiate or try to settle. But the truth was, Mr. Mathers had legal standing, and Danny didn't have a leg to stand on. Freaked out, Danny didn't do anything and ignored the lawsuit. Predictably, Mr. Mathers got a default judgment against Danny. The lawsuit sank him, and he had to close his business. Remember Chapter 6? This is exactly why we don't ignore lawsuits. It's a surefire way to lose before you've even started fighting.

If Danny had included a simple clause in his contract stating that he wasn't responsible for any price increases or labor shortages beyond his control, the story would have turned out completely different. That provision would have shifted the burden to Mr. Mathers. When the cost of materials skyrocketed and workers were impossible to find, Danny could have gone to Mr. Mathers and said, "Look, I'm going to need to charge more, or we can cancel the contract."

If Mr. Mathers had agreed to pay the extra cost, Danny could have kept the job. If he refused, Danny could have walked away without facing a lawsuit, and he'd still have his business today. Even if Mr. Mathers had tried to sue, Danny could've pointed to the contract and said, "I warned you this might happen, and you didn't want to pay more, so that's on you."

But because Danny didn't have that clause, he didn't have that protection—and in the end, it cost him everything.

It's a harsh lesson, but a critical one. When you're dealing with contracts, always plan for the unexpected. You might think the future looks predictable when you sign the deal, but the truth is, things can change fast. And if you're not prepared, those changes can be devastating.

The unfortunate truth is that most residential contracts don't account for unexpected circumstances—things like skyrocketing material prices, labor shortages, or weather delays. If you haven't prepared for these surprises, you could be left footing the bill or, worse, in breach of contract. The solution is simple: Include a provision in your contract that allows for adjustments when unforeseen events happen. This chapter will show you exactly how to do that and why it's essential for protecting your business.

HOW DO YOU PLAN FOR THE UNEXPECTED?

As a contractor, you know the drill: The price you quote and the timeline you promise are based on the reality of that moment. But reality can change fast.

Let's rewind to 2008. Back then, steel prices shot through the roof, and many contractors found themselves scrambling because their contracts didn't include provisions for price increases. Some contractors added these clauses in the aftermath, but as time passed, even the most seasoned professionals forgot the pain. Now, flash forward to 2020, and we saw history repeat itself during the pandemic. The price of materials soared, and many contractors ended up eating those costs because their contracts didn't include language to protect them.

That's why it's important to include language that gives you the ability to pass unexpected costs—like increased material prices—onto the homeowner, and to extend the project timeline when delays occur beyond your control. It's your safety net, ensuring you're not the one paying out of pocket when things in the business change. This provision essentially helps you *cover your ass* for things that are simply out of your control.

You don't want to get stuck paying for extra expenses—and this clause makes sure you don't have to. The key is to include language that clearly states any additional costs resulting from unforeseen events will be covered by the homeowner, not you.

What makes this provision so important? It prepares you for anything. While the pandemic is a once-in-a-generation event, unexpected challenges happen all the time. You can't predict when a hurricane will delay shipments, when labor will be impossible to find, or when a power outage will shut down your worksite. But you *can* prepare for those possibilities by making sure your contract allows for adjustments.

WHAT SHOULD THE PROVISION INCLUDE?

When crafting this provision, think of all the unexpected events that could impact your project. Here are a few you'll want to account for:

1. **Price Increases:** The cost of materials can fluctuate dramatically—whether it's lumber, steel, or even appliances. If you don't have a clause allowing you to adjust the total contract price based on material

costs at the time of purchase, you may find yourself in a position where your profit margin disappears.

2. **Weather Delays:** If rain, freezing temperatures, or other weather-related events prevent you from working, the project timeline should allow for that. The contract should clearly state that delays caused by weather will result in an extension of the completion date.
3. **Labor Shortages:** Finding qualified workers is becoming harder in many regions. If you're facing delays because you can't find enough labor, this provision gives you more time to complete the project without penalty.
4. **Health-Related Delays:** COVID-19 shone a spotlight on how illness can halt a project. If your team gets sick and work stops, your contract should have a provision that allows for extra time to get back on track.
5. **Power Outages:** Whether due to weather or scheduled by utility companies, power outages can throw a wrench in your timeline. Ensure the provision includes these scenarios, so you're not penalized when the lights go out.
6. **Disasters:** Unexpected events like flooding, tornadoes, or even a pipe bursting (like we talked about in the last chapter) can bring work to a halt. The provision should allow for extra time in case of these disasters, so you're not held responsible for delays out of your control.

These specific provisions cover many common scenarios, but no list can anticipate every possible curveball. That's why it's essential to include a general escape clause (Chapter 6) as a safety net. This clause ensures that if something unexpected arises that isn't explicitly listed, you're still protected and have the flexibility to address the situation without penalty.

PROTECTING THE TIMELINE

This provision isn't just about protecting your wallet; it's also about the project schedule. If shipments are delayed or workers are out sick, your project will take longer. Having this clause in place means you can extend the timeline without putting yourself at risk of breaching the contract.

For example, during the pandemic, windows took up to eight weeks to arrive, compared to the usual two or three weeks. With this provision, you can communicate with the homeowner: "The fridge you chose will take ten weeks to get here. If you want to stick with that choice, we'll need to extend the schedule. Otherwise, we can choose a different model that's available sooner." This gives you the flexibility to work with your client while protecting yourself from unreasonable expectations.

EXAMPLE CONTRACT LANGUAGE TO INCLUDE

To make sure you're covered, include contract language like this:

> *In the event of price increases, delays in material shipments, labor shortages, weather-related interruptions, or other unexpected circumstances beyond the contractor's control, the homeowner agrees to cover additional expenses and grant an extension of the project schedule as needed.*

With this clause, you're not just protecting your bottom line—you're also setting clear expectations for the homeowner. They know that if things go wrong (and they often do), it won't come out of your pocket, and the project timeline will reflect the new reality.

KEY TAKEAWAYS

- Make sure to write in protections for yourself for things that you can't control.
- If it's not in the contract, you have to honor the terms exactly as they are.
- Set clear expectations with homeowners, especially about timeline and costs.

PLAN FOR THE UNEXPECTED

Danny's story is a perfect example of what can happen when you don't plan for the unexpected. He never imagined that a pandemic would cause material prices to skyrocket and labor to become scarce, but when it did, he was left without any protections. Because his contract didn't include a provision for price increases or delays, he had no legal standing to renegotiate the terms or walk away without consequence. Ultimately, it cost him not just the job, but his entire business.

As a contractor, you can't control everything—but you can control how prepared you are. This provision is your lifeline when the unexpected happens. Whether it's a global pandemic, a sudden spike in material prices, or just a week of nonstop rain, this clause will keep your project moving forward and your business in the black. Don't let the unexpected catch you off guard. Protect yourself, your business, and your future by including this must-have provision in every contract.

What happens if a client wants out of your contract? Be sure to include language around that in your contract so you can get paid for damages. We cover that next.

CHAPTER 10

CANCELLATION CLAUSE

Contracts are the cornerstone of protecting your business. Yet, many contractors overlook one critical provision that can save them from lengthy legal battles and ensure they're compensated when things go wrong: the cancellation clause. This simple clause can mean the difference between walking away with the profit you've earned or being left high and dry, arguing your case in court.

In this chapter, you'll learn why including a cancellation clause in your contract is essential for protecting your business. We'll cover how this provision ensures you're compensated if a homeowner decides to cancel, and how it prevents lengthy disputes by setting clear, upfront expectations. With the right language in your contract, you can safeguard your profit, simplify potential legal battles, and ensure your time and effort are valued—whether a project is completed or not.

WHAT IS A CANCELLATION CLAUSE?

A cancellation clause is a provision in your contract that clearly defines what happens if the homeowner decides to cancel the project after the agreement is signed. It gives the homeowner the right to cancel the contract, but with a crucial stipulation: *They must compensate you for time, effort, and profit lost* as a result of the cancellation.

It's important to note that, in most states, homeowners are legally entitled to a three-day right to cancel a contract without any penalty. During these three days, the homeowner can back out at no cost, regardless of what's in your contract. However, once that window closes, your cancellation clause kicks in, protecting your right to compensation if they cancel after the grace period.

The most important aspect of a cancellation clause is that it defines, in clear terms, the damages you're entitled to if a project is canceled. These damages generally include the profit you would have made had the project been completed.

Without this clause, you'll face an uphill battle to recover damages.

If a homeowner decides to pull out of a contract, you may have to fight in court to prove what your damages are, including your lost profit. That process can be expensive, stressful, and slow. A cancellation clause sets clear expectations for both parties upfront, ensuring that your rights are protected and that you're fairly compensated.

The truth is, no one wants to go to court to argue over profits. But without a cancellation clause, that's exactly the situation you could find yourself in.

Homeowners sometimes don't understand the gravity of signing a contract and think they can cancel without consequences. A cancellation clause sets the record straight. It informs the homeowner that canceling the contract will cost them something—typically your profit.

PROTECTING YOUR PROFIT

Let's say you've signed a contract, scheduled the project, and maybe even started ordering materials. Then suddenly, the homeowner calls and cancels the contract. What now? Without a cancellation clause, you could be left trying to calculate the profit you're owed, while the homeowner might resist paying anything beyond what they've already given you.

With a cancellation clause, you're better protected. You've already agreed upon the damages for such an event, which typically includes the profit you would have earned had the project been completed. Whether the project is canceled before you start or halfway through, your contract should state what you're entitled to based on the stage of the work.

There are two critical moments in any project where cancellation fees come into play:

1. **Before Work Begins:** If the homeowner cancels before any work starts, you should keep the non-refundable deposit. This compensates you for your time in scheduling, preparing, and potentially turning away other work. A cancellation clause makes it clear that once the contract is signed, the homeowner is committed to either moving forward or forfeiting the deposit. This prevents them from "willy-nilly" canceling without any financial consequences.
2. **After Work Has Begun:** If the homeowner cancels during the project, your contract should state that you're entitled to compensation for the work completed up until the cancellation, plus a percentage of the remaining contract to account for the profit you

would have made. For example, if the total contract is $100,000 and the homeowner has paid $50,000, you are still entitled to a portion of the remaining $50,000 as lost profit—typically a percentage ranging between 10 percent and 50 percent, depending on your pricing model and industry standards.

By setting clear terms in your cancellation clause, you're not just protecting your business—you're simplifying any future legal battles. If a homeowner decides to cancel mid-project, they'll know what they owe you. There's no need to fight over ambiguous figures or argue in court about the value of your work. Instead, the contract has already outlined the compensation you're due.

This clarity saves both time and money, and helps avoid drawn-out disputes.

For larger projects that span months or even a year, I recommend a tiered cancellation clause approach. This allows you to set different cancellation fees based on project milestones. The fees increase as the project progresses, ensuring you're compensated fairly no matter when the project is canceled.

The percentage you charge for lost profit varies depending on the scope of the project and the standard for your specific trade. While some contractors may only charge

10 percent of the remaining contract, others could go as high as 50 percent. This percentage represents the profit you would have earned on the uncompleted work, ensuring that your time, effort, and expertise are fairly compensated.

KEY CONTRACT LANGUAGE TO INCLUDE

To make sure you're covered, include contract language like this:

> In the event the homeowner cancels the contract after signing, the homeowner agrees to compensate the contractor as follows:
> - If cancellation occurs before work has begun, the homeowner forfeits the non-refundable deposit as compensation for time spent on scheduling, preparation, and lost opportunities.
> - If cancellation occurs after work has commenced, the contractor is entitled to payment for all completed work, plus [X] percent of the remaining contract balance as compensation for lost profit. The percentage of compensation may vary depending on the project phase at the time of cancellation.
> - The contractor may seek additional compensation for materials ordered or costs incurred directly related to the project prior to cancellation.

This clause sets clear expectations for both parties, ensuring that if a project is canceled, there is no ambiguity about the contractor's rights to compensation.

> **KEY TAKEAWAYS**
>
> - If you want to get paid for damages in the event your client pulls out of the project, include a cancellation clause.
> - Specify compensation for different stages of each project.
> - Set clear expectations and avoid ambiguity.

VALUE YOUR TIME, PROTECT YOUR BUSINESS

The cancellation clause is an essential safeguard for any contractor. It ensures that if a homeowner cancels a project, you're paid for your time, effort, and lost profit. Without it, you risk lengthy disputes and lost revenue. By clearly outlining your compensation in the event of cancellation, you protect your business from uncertainty and make sure that every project, whether completed or not, values your time and expertise.

Remember: The damages you are entitled to as a contractor are *your profit*. If this isn't built into the contract, you'll have to prove it in court—and nobody wants that.

Avoid potential future disputes on how your work will be judged by including a provision that sets those standards, which we will dive into next.

CHAPTER 11

STANDARDS

Ben had been building decks for more than twenty years, and he prided himself on his craftsmanship. When he got the call from Ms. Parker, a homeowner living in the middle of nowhere, she wanted a simple deck overlooking her vast, rocky landscape. The area was so remote that it didn't require permits, and Ben was more than happy to take on the job.

The project went off without a hitch. Ben completed the deck, ensuring it was sturdy and functional. Ms. Parker seemed satisfied, using the deck regularly without any issues.

But trouble began when Ms. Parker learned from a neighbor from the next county over that the standard in their county required piers to be sunk eight feet deep, not six.

Ms. Parker, now uncertain about the structural integrity of her deck, decided to take the matter to arbitration. She argued that despite the deck's apparent functionality, the piers should have been deeper to meet what she considered a more appropriate standard for the region.

Ben defended his work, pointing out that six feet had always been sufficient in the area and he had never encountered any problems with decks built this way. He even included this depth in his scope of work.

Unfortunately, Ben didn't have a standards clause.

Even though his work was solid and had never failed in similar conditions, the lack of a clear industry standard in his contract left him vulnerable to interpretation. Without a clause in his contract that clearly defined the industry standard or his own practices, the arbitrator ruled in favor of Ms. Parker. She won $18,000, covering the cost of the deck.

As a contractor, you don't want your work judged by a random, unqualified opinion. Yet that's exactly what can happen if you don't clearly define the standards by which your work will be evaluated. In this chapter, we'll explore the importance of including a Standards Clause in your contracts to define how your work will be judged, ensuring clear expectations between you and your clients, protecting your business from subjective opinions, and safeguarding against disputes in court or arbitration.

SETTING THE STANDARDS

A standards clause is a simple yet powerful provision in your contract that can mean the difference between winning and losing a dispute. Think of it as your shield, a way to avoid a client's claim that your work is defective, and more importantly, to ensure your work is judged fairly—not by someone who's making it up as they go, but by the standards you've set.

I'm sure you've been there before: A client claims your work is "defective" and demands their money back. But what are they basing that on? Their gut feeling? A YouTube video they watched? Without standards in your contract, they (or an arbitrator) are free to pull in any "expert" who might have wildly different expectations from what is reasonable.

Including a standards clause puts *you* in control. You set the rules, and you ensure everyone's playing the same game—your game. And if things go south and end up in court or arbitration, this clause is your lifeline.

THE POWER OF DEFINING YOUR OWN STANDARDS

Say you're a painting contractor. You've done a great job, but your client is standing two inches from the wall, nitpicking every tiny flaw. "There's a little bump here, and I don't like the texture over there." But professional standards, like those from the Painting Contractors Association (PCA), say you should evaluate the paint job from *four feet* away. That's the industry standard.

With a standards clause referencing the PCA, you can confidently tell your client, "Look, the work meets the standards." And guess what? Those are the standards that will prevail in court. You're not at the mercy of a client's emotions or unrealistic expectations. This is why setting your own standards—whether for painting, tiling, or framing—matters so much.

This need becomes even more crucial when we talk about remodeling. Remodelers deal with a wide range of tasks—plumbing, lighting, concrete work, and more. Inspectors for each of these tasks will focus on specific elements of the job, often judging it by strict standards that may differ from general building standards. Concrete inspectors will nitpick your foundation, while AC inspectors scrutinize your ductwork. But if you've laid out the general standards in your contract, you give yourself some breathing room.

Let's take masonry as an example. Mixing mortar is an

art form, but no matter how consistent you are, slight variations in color can occur. If you've had clients in the past complain about this, it's essential to set that expectation up front—and include it in your standards clause: "Mortar color may vary slightly depending on the mix." By including this language, you're defining what's acceptable and avoiding disputes over things you can't fully control.

KEEP IT SIMPLE

Including a standards clause in your contract doesn't have to be overwhelming or complicated. In fact, it can be as simple as providing a URL or a link to the relevant standards. You don't need to rewrite pages of industry regulations into your contract—just point your clients to where they can find the details.

For example, if you're a painting contractor, you could reference the PCA standards and include a link to their website. If you're a remodeler, you might use the National Association of Home Builders (NAHB) or even your local building code. In California, it's even easier because the state has specific rules for different types of contractors. You can simply refer to the California regulations that apply to your trade and include a link to those in your contract. For instance, if you're an HVAC contractor, you can reference the California Building Energy Efficiency

Standards, or if you're a plumbing contractor, you can include the California Plumbing Code.

By adding a simple link, you're making it clear to your client that these are the standards your work will be judged by. It takes the guesswork out of the equation and ensures everyone is on the same page from the start. When disputes arise, you'll have something concrete to back you up, and your work will be measured against established benchmarks rather than subjective opinions.

So, don't overthink it. The standards clause doesn't require a lot of extra work—it's a straightforward line in your contract with a link to the relevant standards. And best of all, it's a simple way to protect your business and avoid costly disputes without overwhelming you or your client.

And while this is obvious, I'm going to say it anyway: Please read and be familiar with the standards you're setting for yourself. If you're going to include a link to the PCA standards or the California building code in your contract, take a little time to read them. You don't need to memorize them like you're prepping for an exam, but you should know the standards. You wouldn't want to end up in court realizing you've been holding yourself to a standard you didn't even know you agreed to.

WHY INSPECTIONS AREN'T THE GOLD STANDARD

You might be thinking, "Well, I pulled the permit, so I'm covered, right?" Wrong. Permits are great for showing that you're in compliance with local building codes, but that doesn't mean your work can't be deemed defective.

Here's the kicker: The county inspector takes no liability for whether the work is done correctly. So just because you passed inspection doesn't mean the inspector's approval will save you if a dispute arises.

A permit is merely evidence that you followed the rules of the municipality—it's not a get-out-of-jail-free card. If you really want to protect yourself, you need a standards clause that clearly states what standards your work will be judged by. That way, you're not leaving anything up to chance or someone else's interpretation of what "good" looks like.

> **KEY TAKEAWAYS**
>
> - Set your standards so your work is not based on whatever standards the owner wants to set.
> - It doesn't have to be complicated; just include the URL.
> - Be familiar with the standards set in your own contract.

SET YOUR STANDARDS

If you don't set the standards, someone else will—and that someone is probably not going to have your best interests at heart. Just ask Ben, the contractor who built a perfectly functional deck but lost an $18,000 arbitration battle because he didn't specify his own standards in the contract. He let someone else decide what "acceptable" meant, and it cost him big time.

By including a standards clause in your contract, you take control of how your work is judged. You set the rules, and you give your clients a clear understanding of what they can expect. It's a win-win. Your clients know they're getting quality work, and if a dispute does arise, you've got a solid foundation to stand on—one built with standards you've chosen.

Up next: warranties. Most states offer implied warranties, but they may be more than what you'd like. Offer the warranties you want to offer by including them in your contract, which we'll cover in the next chapter.

CHAPTER 12

WARRANTIES

Meet Sean, a contractor who completed a $30,000 whole-house window replacement job for his client, Mr. Knight. Sean had done everything by the book: He'd installed the windows, ensured they were functioning properly, and even had a contract clause that specified the client had to pay the balance in full, minus 3 percent for any punch list items, once the job was complete. Mr. Knight had paid a $3,000 deposit, but the remaining $27,000 was still outstanding.

After the windows were installed, there were a few minor issues—scuff marks here, a window that felt a little tight there. Nothing major, and certainly not enough to justify withholding payment. Sean even brought the window manufacturer out to confirm that the issues were minor and could be easily addressed. But Mr. Knight wasn't satisfied. He kept nitpicking and refusing to pay the balance, stalling at every opportunity.

I'm sure you've experienced this before, too.

Frustrated but determined, Sean took a bold step. His contract clearly stated that the windows still technically belonged to him until the full payment was made, so he removed the hardware that allowed the windows to open. Mr. Knight was left with brand-new, perfectly installed windows that he couldn't open. After a few weeks of back-and-forth, Mr. Knight finally realized that opening his windows was more important than dragging out the argument. He paid the remaining $27,000, and Sean promptly fixed the minor issues, just as his warranty promised.

The moral of the story? A well-written warranty (and a solid contract) can be your best friend when things get tough.

In this chapter, you'll learn why a warranty is more than just a promise to fix things—it's a tool that protects your business, helps manage client expectations, and ensures you get paid. We'll dive into how to craft a warranty that sets clear rules for how your work will be judged, so you can avoid endless liabilities and sleep easier at night.

WARRANTIES 101: THE BASICS

Warranties—every contractor knows they need one, but not everyone fully understands just how important they really are. At its core, a warranty is your legal obligation to repair or replace defective work or materials within a certain period after completing the project.

For residential construction contracts, there are two types: express and implied.

Express warranties are those promises you explicitly make to your clients—whether they're in the contract, on your website, or something you said over coffee. If you promise your work will stand up to a certain standard, that's an express warranty, and you're obligated to follow through. For example, if you tell your client, "This deck will last for ten years without any issues," that's an express warranty.

Implied warranties, on the other hand, are not based on anything you say or write. These are built into the law, whether you mention them or not. They exist because of the nature of the work itself. A common example is the implied warranty of habitability—if you build a house, it's implied that it should be fit to live in. Even if you don't spell this out, it's assumed. It's implied that a roof will keep water out is another example. Implied warranties can be tricky because they exist whether you write them into your contract or not.

The key point I'd like to emphasize is this: Both express and implied warranties are automatically there, whether you like it or not. But don't let that freak you out. You can limit your liability by clearly defining your express warranties in your contract.

This is where a well-written contract comes in.

LIMITING WARRANTIES WITH CONTRACT LANGUAGE

To avoid being held to overly broad expectations, your contract should spell out exactly what warranties you are providing—and nothing more. For example, you can add a simple clause like:

"The only warranties provided are those explicitly stated in this contract. No verbal promises made outside of this agreement will be honored."

You can also limit implied warranties by adding clear language to your contract. If you prefer not to offer implied warranties, include a clause like this:

"All implied warranties, including warranties of merchant-

ability and fitness for a particular purpose, are disclaimed to the fullest extent allowed by law."

And if you're in one of those states that doesn't allow you to sell work "as is," such as Connecticut or Massachusetts, be sure to know the laws before trying to exclude implied warranties.

This keeps things clean and manageable. You control what's covered, and there's no room for misinterpretation.

THE BIG RULE: NO WARRANTY UNTIL FULL PAYMENT

Here's a critical rule you should live by: *Warranties don't start until you've been paid in full.* This should be written in your contract, plain and simple. It protects you from clients who want to drag out payments over every little scuff mark or minor issue. For example, you could include a clause like this:

"All work is warranted for one year from the date of completion. However, no warranty will apply until full payment is received."

This ensures that clients can't take advantage of you, while still giving them peace of mind that their work is protected once they settle the bill.

Another important detail to include in your warranty clause is who decides how issues are addressed. Make it clear that *you, the contractor, have the sole discretion to determine whether something is repaired or replaced under the warranty*. This protects you from unreasonable demands, like clients insisting on a full replacement when a simple repair would suffice.

By clearly defining the terms of your warranty—including when it starts and how issues are resolved—you set firm boundaries, protect your business, and avoid unnecessary disputes.

MAINTENANCE VS. DEFECTS: KNOW THE DIFFERENCE

Another key part of managing warranties is defining what's considered a defect versus what's just poor maintenance. Let's say you install landscaping, and the client doesn't water the plants. If those plants die, that's not your fault, therefore not your problem—it's a maintenance issue. But if the client claims it's defective work, you could end up in an argument that's difficult to resolve.

Include language in your contract that says you as the contractor will determine whether an issue is due to a defect in the work or a lack of proper maintenance. You could write something like:

"The contractor will determine whether an issue is a result of defective work or inadequate maintenance. The homeowner is responsible for maintaining the property according to the contractor's guidelines."

This protects you from being blamed for things outside your control.

EXTRA TIPS FOR STRENGTHENING YOUR WARRANTIES

A solid warranty can protect your business and set clear expectations, but there are additional steps you can take to reinforce your contract and avoid future headaches. The following represent two extra considerations for you:

1. **Offer Maintenance Contracts:** If your work requires ongoing upkeep, consider offering a maintenance contract as an add-on. For example, if you install exterior stucco that needs to be cleaned regularly, you can provide a yearly contract to come out and maintain it for a fee. This keeps the client happy, ensures their manufacturer warranty stays valid, and helps you avoid future disputes over poorly maintained installations.
2. **Don't Forget Your Subcontractors:** If you're working with subcontractors, make sure they provide you with the same warranties that you offer to your clients.

Get it in writing that the subcontractor will warrant their work for at least a year. This way, if something goes wrong, you're not left holding the bag, and you have legal recourse to ensure that any defects are corrected without affecting your client relationship.

> **KEY TAKEAWAYS**
>
> - Specify exactly what is covered under your warranty and what is not so there is no room for misinterpretation.
> - Don't honor the warranty until your work is paid in full.
> - Make it clear in your contract what constitutes a defect versus a maintenance issue, so you're not held responsible for problems caused by poor upkeep.

PROTECT YOURSELF

Warranties are a powerful tool in your toolbox, but only if they're written correctly. Without a proper warranty, you're leaving yourself exposed to unexpected liabilities and client demands. But with a solid warranty in place, like our window installer, you set the rules for how your work will be judged. When the homeowner tried to withhold payment, Sean was able to fall back on his warranty clause—no payment, no warranty. In the end, Mr. Knight paid up, and Sean honored his promise by fixing the minor issues.

By writing a clear, specific warranty in your contract, you can protect yourself, limit your liability, and control the narrative of what happens if things go wrong. Make sure your warranty covers what you intend it to, and always—*always*—get paid in full before the warranty kicks in.

And disputes are going to happen! We'll explore what you can do to cover your ass in the next chapter.

CHAPTER 13

DISPUTES

Kelly had been in the contracting business for over a decade and had worked hard to establish a solid reputation—or so he thought. He figured his clients respected his work, even if they sometimes grumbled about minor issues. So, when he finished a $100,000 home remodel for the Martins, he assumed they were satisfied. They'd had some complaints along the way, sure—cracks in the drywall, uneven paint on a bedroom wall—but Kelly was used to handling those kinds of issues without fuss. When Mrs. Martin brought up these issues, he gave her a vague, "I'll take care of it," and moved on. In his mind, no news was good news, and he brushed off any further comments.

A month after the job wrapped up, though, Kelly received an official-looking envelope: a demand letter from the

Martins. They were unhappy with several aspects of the project and claimed he had left defects in the work.

Defective work? Kelly thought to himself. *Please.*

The letter got buried under invoices and receipts on his desk, and he went about his business, assuming the Martins would just let it go.

Thirty days later, Kelly received another envelope, this time with "Notice of Lawsuit" printed in bold. Now he was really annoyed. He threw the letter aside, grumbling to himself about ungrateful clients and dismissing the idea of responding. In Kelly's mind, he'd done excellent work. The Martins were just being difficult. He figured if he ignored it long enough, the whole thing would blow over.

It didn't.

Several months later, Kelly got a final piece of mail—this one notifying him of a judgment entered against him for the Martins' full claim: $100,000 plus attorney's fees. Now Kelly's jaw dropped. They had won the case, and he hadn't even gotten the chance to defend himself. Panicking, he called me hoping for a miracle.

"Well, Kelly," I said after reading through the judgment,

"I'm going to be honest. There's not much we can do here. You had multiple chances to respond, and each time you ignored it, you dug yourself in deeper. The courts gave you a thirty-day window after the judgment to try and reopen the case, but now…it's been over a year."

Kelly slumped in his chair, hardly believing his ears. "So… what happens now?" he asked.

"It's not good," I said, "Now the Martins can go after your assets. That means bank accounts, wages, property, even your personal belongings if they can justify it. They can garnish your wages too. And unless we can work out a payment plan, they'll keep coming after whatever assets they can get their hands on until the full amount is paid."

Kelly felt his stomach drop.

Reluctantly, Kelly agreed to work out a plan with the Martins' attorney. In the end, he committed to $2,500 a month until the debt was paid off. It was a painful arrangement, but the only option left. As he made his first payment, he couldn't help but think about that first demand letter—the one he'd tossed aside with a shrug.

IT'S ONLY A MATTER OF TIME

In life, there are very few guarantees: death, taxes, and, if you're a residential contractor, disputes. It's not a question of *if* they'll happen; it's a question of *when*.

As much as it pains me to say it, you should go into every job with the mindset that things could end in a dispute. No, it's not fun. But this mindset will force you to implement strategies that cover your ass. When a problem does pop up, you'll be glad you took the time to protect yourself.

Construction is inherently unpredictable; even with the best planning, something might not turn out as expected, or a client might just not like how something looks. The goal here isn't to hand over the keys to the kingdom—it's to communicate and manage expectations.

Disputes don't always come from a homeowner, either. Sometimes you'll be the one who has to file a complaint, like when a client doesn't pay up.

Believe it or not, most disputes can be resolved well before they turn into full-blown nightmares. Problems arise when contractors don't respond to issues, avoid communication, or fail to make a plan of action.

In this chapter, you'll learn how to effectively handle

disputes before they escalate, why timely communication and proper documentation are your best defenses, and how implementing strategies like arbitration and digital tools can help safeguard your business and prevent legal battles like the one that blindsided Kelly.

DON'T IGNORE COMPLAINTS

If there's one thing you take away from this chapter, let it be this: *Don't ignore client complaints.*

If they bring up an issue, address it, document it, and move on. If it's something outside the original contract, fill out a change order and adjust the price or timeline as needed. Even if there's no immediate dispute, keeping thorough records of all communications helps if issues escalate. If a larger conflict arises, you'll have evidence of how smaller problems were resolved, which helps you respond effectively and reasonably.

Another tip? Address every complaint promptly. Homeowners often let little annoyances pile up, and if they feel unheard, those small issues snowball until one big problem sets them off. Suddenly, you're hit with a list of complaints, some of which you thought were long resolved. By that time, it's hard to get things back on track without tempers flaring and letters flying. Document every exchange, even minor grievances, so you can point back to how things were handled. This paper trail is invaluable if a client brings up old complaints as unresolved later on.

There are plenty of opportunities for you to resolve disputes. We went over the stages briefly in Chapter 6, but it is worth repeating here. The following represent how most disputes progress and how to nip them in the bud:

1. **Prevention Stage:** Most disputes start with minor complaints. A homeowner may ask about small issues or seem unhappy with something. This is the time to address it, document it, and prevent things from escalating.
2. **Demand Letter Stage:** If the problem continues, it may escalate to a demand letter. In about a dozen states, contractors have a "right to cure," meaning they get the opportunity to fix a problem before a lawsuit is filed. Whether or not your state requires it, this is a good standard practice to adopt and implement. The most important thing for you to do if you receive a demand letter is to respond. A demand letter without a response will be Exhibit A in court, painting you as unresponsive and irresponsible.
3. **Lawsuit Stage:** If disputes escalate to lawsuits, you're looking at a drawn-out process with significant time and costs. Even at this stage, however, it is possible to settle out of court. However, if your case

goes to trial, remember that judges or juries will often sympathize with homeowners over contractors. This is why having a documented paper trail, solid communication, and clear contract terms are crucial to protecting your business.

Addressing issues early and often can help you avoid demand letters and lawsuits. When in doubt, communicate clearly and often with your homeowners.

Overcommunication might feel excessive, but trust me, it's your best friend. Every text, email, and photo can be a crucial piece of evidence if a project goes south. This isn't just about making clients happy—it's about having proof of all interactions, decisions, and outcomes if you ever end up in court.

TIPS FOR AVOIDING DISPUTES

Here are some tips to keep disputes at bay and protect yourself if things start to go sideways:

1. **Have a Clear Contract:** This should be obvious by now: Set expectations from the start with a contract that both you and your client understand. It's your foundation for dealing with issues.
2. **Document Everything:** Use digital tools like apps or software to keep all emails, texts, photos, and change

orders organized by project. Platforms like JobTread allow you to store communication, contracts, invoices, and photos in one place, making it easy to stay on top of everything. (More about technology coming up).
3. **Overcommunicate:** Be over the top when it comes to addressing concerns. If a client has a problem, respond promptly, address it, and check in afterward to make sure they're happy. A lack of communication is often what leads to disputes, as homeowners begin to fill in blanks with inaccurate stories that they tell themselves.
4. **Keep a Paper Trail:** For every issue, create a complete documentation cycle: Record the problem, outline the agreed-upon solution, document the fix, and capture the client's acknowledgment (where possible). Even a quick "all good" from the client after an issue is resolved helps reinforce your side.
5. **Consider Arbitration:** An arbitration clause ensures that disputes are handled by an expert and kept out of public court, giving you a more favorable setting to present your side (more on this in a minute).
6. **Don't Be Afraid to Offer a Little Extra:** Sometimes, offering more than you're comfortable with (within reason) can help you move on and focus on new projects. It's better to spend a bit now and move forward than to pay big bucks fighting a battle over past work.

EMBRACING TECHNOLOGY

If you're still avoiding tech, here's your cue to change that and get on board.

The construction industry has been late to the game when it comes to incorporating technology into the business, but digital tools have never been more accessible or affordable. Many platforms let you manage the entire project lifecycle, from contracts to change orders to client communication.

Let's be real: Most contractors don't like change, especially when it involves learning new technology. Why switch up what's worked for years? But the truth is, staying old-school can leave you more exposed than you realize. Adopting tech tools may feel like a pain in the short term, but the benefits are massive. And once you're set up, the ease of managing projects, tracking communication, and keeping records will make you wonder why you didn't do it sooner.

Here's what embracing technology can do for you:

1. **Documentation, Documentation, Documentation:** When disputes arise, it's all about having proof. Technology makes it effortless to keep a digital paper trail—every email, text, change order, and even photos can be stored in one place. Platforms

like JobTread let you upload these files to specific projects, making it easy to reference later if issues come up. A quick search lets you pull up a timeline of every communication and every document, which can be a lifesaver if there's a dispute.

2. **Instant Communication with Clients:** Clear communication is key to keeping homeowners happy and stopping their imaginations from running wild. With digital platforms, you can send updates, share schedules, and notify clients of any changes in real time. Many platforms even allow clients to log in and view project progress, which means fewer calls, fewer "what's going on?" messages, and a happier, well-informed homeowner.

3. **Efficient Project Management:** From tracking tasks to assigning jobs to different team members, construction management software gives you a bird's-eye view of every project in one place. Instead of juggling phone calls, sticky notes, or a cluttered calendar, you have everything organized in a single dashboard. Need to check if the electrician has completed wiring? Or confirm when materials are arriving? It's all there in one click.

4. **Easily Create and Store Contracts:** Let's face it: Carrying around a clipboard with contracts in the truck can get messy. With digital tools, you can upload your contracts, share them with clients, and even collect e-signatures, making the process quick

and secure. Some platforms also store templates, so when it's time for a new project, you can just pull up a saved contract, adjust for the new job, and send it out. No more lost paperwork or time wasted searching for documents.

5. **Financial Tracking and Job Costing:** Most management platforms allow you to track expenses and payments in real time. From tracking job costs to managing invoices and change orders, these platforms give you an up-to-date view of your financials. Some even sync directly with accounting software like QuickBooks, making tax season a whole lot smoother and giving you a crystal-clear view of each project's profitability.

6. **Change Orders on the Spot:** Change orders can be a headache, especially if you're still trying to handle them on paper. With an iPad or phone, you can make adjustments on the spot, get digital approval, and instantly add them to the project timeline and budget. It keeps clients in the loop and saves you the hassle of going back to the office, typing up documents, and chasing down signatures.

7. **Keeps Everyone Accountable:** Technology doesn't just make your life easier—it keeps everyone, from subcontractors to suppliers to clients, on the same page. With centralized communication and a shared project timeline, everyone knows what's expected of them, when it's due, and what needs to happen

next. And if someone doesn't deliver, you've got the records to prove it, protecting you from any finger-pointing down the line.
8. **Access Anywhere, Any Time:** One of the biggest perks of tech tools is mobility. With a tablet or phone, you can check job progress, communicate with clients, or even sign a contract without stepping foot in the office. You're no longer tied to paper files or a desktop computer, meaning you can stay on top of things wherever you are, whether you're on the job site, in the truck, or even on vacation (although, fingers crossed, that one's rare).

I know making the leap into tech can be intimidating. Construction is a hands-on industry, and you may feel more comfortable with tools you can hold than apps you can download. But think of technology as just another tool in your toolkit—one designed to protect your work, save time, and streamline every aspect of the job.

If you're worried about complexity, start with just one feature, like digital contracts or photo documentation. Once you get comfortable, you can build from there. And remember, you don't have to do this alone. Many platforms offer tutorials or customer support to help you get started.

The industry is shifting, and technology is becoming the

standard for contractors who want to stay competitive, efficient, and protected. So, give it a try, and see the difference it can make in simplifying your processes and securing your business. In a world where disputes are inevitable, this is one change that's definitely worth it.

THE BENEFITS OF ARBITRATION

For many contractors, adding an arbitration clause to contracts is a game-changer. Arbitration is a form of private dispute resolution where an arbitrator—usually a construction industry expert—reviews the case and makes a binding decision. Unlike court, where judges and juries often lack construction expertise, an arbitrator understands the ins and outs of your work.

I recommend including an arbitration clause in your contract for several reasons:

- **Privacy:** Arbitration is a private process, meaning no public record exists of the dispute, unlike a court case.
- **Efficiency:** Though it has upfront costs, arbitration saves time and money in the long run because the process is faster than a public trial.
- **Expertise:** Arbitrators are often construction lawyers or industry professionals, making their judgments informed by real experience rather than general knowledge.

To include arbitration in your contract, you must have a written agreement that both parties agree to arbitration instead of a court trial in case of a dispute. It's an upfront investment but one that could save you substantial costs and headaches down the road.

> **KEY TAKEAWAYS**
>
> - Don't ignore complaints or demand letters. A judgment can be taken against you by default if you ignore them.
> - Embrace technology for better project management.
> - Use arbitration to keep disputes out of court.

PLAN FOR THE BEST, PREPARE FOR THE WORST

Kelly's story is a harsh reminder that ignoring disputes won't make them go away—in fact, it only makes them worse. By dismissing the Martins' complaints and failing to respond to the demand letter, Kelly allowed a minor issue to snowball into a full-blown lawsuit, costing him $100,000 and threatening his livelihood. If Kelly had taken the time to address the Martins' concerns early on, or even responded to the initial demand letter, he could have steered the situation toward a more favorable outcome.

As much as we'd like to avoid conflict, addressing issues head-on and keeping thorough records can make all the difference. Be proactive, overcommunicate, and, if a dispute does arise, remember you have options. Arbitration, demand letters, and negotiation give you a framework to handle issues professionally and fairly.

Disputes are inevitable in construction, but by preparing for them, you can protect yourself, your reputation, and your business. Approach each project with the mentality that disputes *could* happen, and you'll set up safeguards that save you time and money down the road.

We've talked at length about covering your ass within the scope of the project, but what about other provisions you may want to include? We'll cover that in the next chapter.

CHAPTER 14

ADDITIONAL PROVISIONS

Wyatt had been in the pond maintenance business long enough to know that sometimes, things go wrong. But nothing could have prepared him for this particular job.

The homeowners had a stunning pond filled with vibrant koi fish—beautiful, expensive creatures that were the pride of the backyard. Wyatt's task was simple: Clean the pond. It seemed like a routine job.

He and his crew carefully removed the fish, cleaned the pond, scrubbed the rocks, and replaced the water, making sure everything was in tip-top shape before returning the fish to their home. It was all in a day's work. But something was off. A few days later, Wyatt received a frantic call from the homeowners: All the fish had died.

Wyatt's heart sank.

The homeowners were devastated, and understandably so. They had invested thousands of dollars in those fish, and now they were gone. Wyatt rushed over to see what had gone wrong, but the damage had already been done. The water chemistry had somehow been thrown off during the cleaning process, and the fish didn't survive the change.

In their contract, Wyatt had been clear that his job was simply to clean the pond. He wasn't responsible for ensuring the fish's survival after the process, as pond maintenance can sometimes cause temporary imbalances in the water chemistry. But the homeowners were understandably upset and wanted compensation—$5,000 to be exact, for the value of the fish they lost.

Wyatt was caught in a tough spot. He had only charged them $3,000 for the cleaning, and now they were asking for more than that in damages. He could have fought it, pointing to the terms of the contract. But in the interest of avoiding a prolonged conflict, Wyatt made a decision: He refunded them the entire $3,000 they had paid for the job. It wasn't the $5,000 they were asking for, but it was enough to settle the issue without going to court or dragging things out.

From this experience, Wyatt added detailed clauses about the risks of water chemistry imbalances and the potential consequences for aquatic life to his future contracts.

In this chapter, we will explore the importance of adding specific provisions to your contracts, using real-life lessons learned by contractors like Wyatt. We'll discuss how these provisions, from limiting liability for consequential damages to addressing potential disputes over social media use, can protect your business from unforeseen complications and strengthen your agreements with clients. By continually updating your contract to reflect new challenges on each project, you'll be better prepared to safeguard your professional reputation and avoid unnecessary liability.

MAKE IT YOUR OWN

Every job teaches you something. Every mistake, every unexpected twist, every moment you find yourself saying, *"Well, I didn't see that coming"*—those are golden opportunities to improve your contract. I always tell my clients, whatever pain points you've experienced in the past—those little headaches you never want to deal with again—make sure you put them in your contract.

After you complete each job, ask yourself: *What lesson did I learn this time?* Did something go sideways? Was there a misunderstanding that could've been avoided? Every project is a learning experience, and the goal is to make sure you don't learn the same lesson twice. Your contract should evolve just like your business does. Contracts aren't static—*they're living, breathing documents* that should be updated regularly. This is how your contract becomes uniquely yours, shaped by the challenges you've faced and the solutions you've come up with.

I can't tell you which provisions you should add to your contract because that will differ depending on what type of work you do. But to give you an idea, here are three examples of provisions contractors have added to their contracts based on lessons learned the hard way:

1. SOCIAL MEDIA USE PROVISION

You've put in the hard work, and naturally, you want to show it off. Showcasing project photos in your portfolio is a great way to attract new clients, but there's a crucial step you can't skip: getting the homeowner's permission. That's why many contractors make it a point to include a clause in their contracts that grants them the right to use photos of the completed work.

Even with this permission, however, situations can change. Maybe the homeowner was excited about showing off their new space at first, but six months later, they've decided they want those pictures taken down for privacy reasons. Sure, you have the legal right to keep them up, but sometimes the smart move is to honor their request. Taking the photos down can go a long way toward maintaining goodwill and showing that you respect their privacy. At the end of the day, being flexible and considerate can do more for your reputation than any single photo ever could.

2. MEDIATION BEFORE BAD REVIEWS PROVISION

Let's be real—reviews can make or break your business. Before a client goes off and posts a scathing review online, you could have a clause in your contract that requires them to try mediation first.

This gives you a chance to address and resolve any issues privately before they become public. If they skip mediation and head straight to social media, it's considered a breach of contract, and you can take action. This approach not only protects your reputation, but also shows that you're committed to resolving problems in a constructive, professional manner. It's a win–win for everyone involved.

3. SPRAY FOAM INSULATION PROVISION

Spray foam insulation can be a fantastic product, but it's not a universal fix. You might install it flawlessly, but if the house isn't set up to handle it properly—like lacking adequate ventilation or having combustible appliances in the attic—it can lead to serious safety issues.

As a contractor, your job is to install the spray foam, not redesign the home's systems. That's why smart contractors include a clause in their contracts stating they're not responsible for how well the spray foam integrates with the home's existing setup. This extra layer of protection is crucial, especially when homeowners, eager for energy savings, don't realize they could be trapping dangerous gasses like carbon monoxide from a water heater or furnace. You don't want to be liable for that kind of risk!

THE CATCH-ALL PHRASE

If there's one line every contractor should absolutely have in their contract, it's this:

"I am not responsible for any consequential damages that arise from the scope of work."

This one sentence is your golden shield. It covers a whole range of potential problems, giving you some serious protection. With this catch-all phrase, you don't need to list out every possible scenario where things could go sideways. It's a powerful line that essentially says, "If something goes wrong that's a natural consequence of the work I'm doing, I'm not liable for the fallout."

Let's break that down a bit. Say a client calls you up, upset because your heavy trucks cracked their driveway while delivering materials. You point to this catch-all phrase in your contract and explain that cracking the driveway is a natural consequence of heavy trucks being necessary for the job. With that phrase, you're not on the hook for fixing the driveway because it's something that could reasonably be expected given the scope of work.

Another example: Say you're tearing out old kitchen tile, and afterward, the homeowner complains that their air vents are clogged with dust. You can say, "Of course your air vents are dusty! I was breaking up tile. But, per our contract, I'm not responsible for cleaning or replacing your HVAC system afterward." As long as you can connect the issue to the natural consequences of your work, you're in the clear.

The following are some common examples where this clause can protect you. It's also a good idea to include these specific provisions in your contract to ensure everything is completely covered:

1. **Escaped Pets:** Construction zones aren't exactly pet-friendly, and sometimes gates get left open, or fences don't hold up. If the homeowner's pets escape during the project, that's not on you. Make sure the homeowner knows it's their responsibility to keep their pets safely secured while work is being done.
2. **Landscaping Damage:** Flower beds and shrubs may look lovely, but they often fall victim to construction projects. Whether it's from the placement of equipment or workers trampling through, unintentional damage can happen. By stating that you're not responsible for replacing or repairing landscaping, you avoid paying for an impromptu gardening session.
3. **Visitors in the Construction Zone:** Homeowners love to show off their in-progress projects to friends and family, but bringing people into an active construction zone is a recipe for disaster. Make it clear in your contract that no one should be wandering around before the project is complete, and if they do, you're not liable for any injuries that occur.
4. **Noise and Vibration:** Construction noise can shake things up—literally. Vibrations from roof work or exterior repairs can cause items to fall off shelves or pictures to rattle off walls. Unless you've been negligent, you shouldn't be held responsible for damages caused by these vibrations. Make sure that's covered in your contract.
5. **Internet Outages:** These days, almost everyone

works from home, which means an unexpected internet outage can be a major inconvenience. If your crew accidentally knocks out the homeowner's internet connection, your contract should clearly state that you're not responsible for any loss of business or work interruptions that result from it.
6. **Delays Leading to Extra Rent or Mortgage Costs:** Sometimes, construction delays are inevitable. If a project runs late, it can cause extra costs for homeowners, especially if they're living in temporary housing or paying additional interest on construction financing. Your contract needs to outline that you're not responsible for these costs if the delay is caused by factors outside of your control. Otherwise, you might find yourself facing a hefty bill.

In short, the catch-all phrase is there to protect you from the endless "what-ifs" that come with construction projects. You can't plan for everything, but you can protect yourself from being held responsible for things that are out of your hands. By clearly outlining what you're *not* liable for, you set clear expectations and shield your business from unexpected expenses.

DODGED A BULLET: WHEN NEGLECT LEADS TO TRAGEDY

Jason had built plenty of backyard ponds in his career, and this one was no different. A beautiful water feature, complete with a waterfall and colorful koi fish, became the crown jewel of the homeowner's outdoor space. The family loved it, and so did their retriever, Max, who enjoyed lounging beside it, watching the fish swim by.

But as time went on, the homeowners neglected the regular maintenance the pond required. A year passed, and the once-pristine water had become murky and stagnant. Algae built up, and bacteria likely began to thrive in the neglected water. One hot afternoon, Max, in his usual carefree manner, drank from the pond.

The family didn't think much of it until Max became gravely ill. Within a couple of days, he passed away. Devastated and searching for answers, they realized that the unclean water in the pond might have been the cause. The homeowners contacted Jason, informing him of what had happened.

Jason was heartbroken. He remembered installing the pond and making sure it was perfect when he left the job a year ago. He had no reason to believe that something like this could happen. But the sad truth was that pond maintenance is crucial—something he'd advised the homeowners about when the job was completed.

While the homeowners were grieving, they didn't blame Jason. They admitted that they hadn't kept up with the maintenance Jason had recommended. Still, that didn't lessen the emotional weight of the situation. Jason offered his sincere condolences and even offered to help with the costs of a new dog, but the family declined. They were simply heartbroken, not looking for money or compensation.

Jason realized how close he had come to a much bigger problem. Although the family didn't hold him responsible, if they had chosen to sue, he could have faced serious legal and financial consequences. His contract at the time didn't include any clauses to protect him from such situations.

It was one helluva wake-up call.

From that point forward, Jason made sure to include a clause in his contracts that clearly stated he wasn't responsible for issues arising from a lack of maintenance. He also began to emphasize the importance of regular pond upkeep to all his clients, explaining how quickly things can go wrong when a water feature is neglected.

It was a hard, tragic lesson, but Jason walked away knowing he had dodged a bullet. While the homeowners didn't take legal action, he knew he needed to protect himself better in the future—because not every client would be as understanding in a situation like this.

> **KEY TAKEAWAYS**
>
> - Adapt and regularly update your contract based on your personal experiences.
> - Clearly outline what you are and aren't responsible for, such as maintenance, consequential damages, and potential disruptions, to shield yourself from unexpected claims.

BE PROACTIVE

Wyatt's and Jason's stories illustrate a vital lesson for contractors: No matter how careful you are, unexpected issues can arise, and they can cost you more than just money. Whether it's a maintenance oversight or a miscommunication about the scope of work, the right contract provisions can protect your business and provide clear guidelines for handling these situations. Contracts should be living documents, evolving with each project and experience, ensuring you learn from past challenges and are better prepared for future ones. By including specific clauses tailored to your line of work, you can avoid unnecessary disputes, maintain strong client relationships, and safeguard your professional reputation.

Once the work is officially done, we want to get paid our last payment. Unfortunately, this process can be problematic. In the next chapter, we'll go over how to streamline this with a punch out process.

CHAPTER 15

PUNCH-OUT PROCESS

You're on the sixth call from a homeowner about some minuscule detail. A light switch feels "off" or a cabinet needs a slight adjustment. You fix it, only to get another call days later. And then another. It starts feeling less like a home improvement project and more like a never-ending saga of small tweaks that never seem to satisfy.

Worse, that last chunk of payment you've been counting on remains just out of reach. The project went over time and over budget, and now you're stuck in a cycle of "fix one more thing" while the homeowner seems to be stalling.

Sound familiar?

It's a game many play to avoid making that final payment. But the good news is, you don't have to play along. In this chapter, we'll show you how to avoid the trap of the never-ending punch-out list by setting expectations early and taking control of the final stage of the job.

THE PUNCH-OUT PROCESS

Every contractor knows what the punch-out process is. It's that final stage of a project where you address those last tweaks, touch-ups, and fixes before calling it a wrap.

But while you surely understand this process, most homeowners don't understand it at all.

For them, it's not just the end—it's a chance to spot every tiny imperfection and keep you on the hook indefinitely. This disconnect can lead to headaches, delays, and a frustrating cycle of endless requests, especially if you're dealing with homeowners going through their first construction project.

The reality is that without a clear understanding of the punch-out process, homeowners might expect the project to be flawless the moment you walk out the door. They might not realize that final adjustments are a normal part of any construction job. Worse yet, some homeowners might use this misunderstanding to stall on making the last payment. Maybe the project went over budget, or it took longer than expected, and now they're hesitant to settle up. Some might even hope you'll get frustrated and walk away without chasing that final check.

But let's make something very clear: You deserve to get paid fully for the work you've done—every last dollar. And the way to ensure that is to be clear from the start. Before the project kicks off, have a sit-down with the homeowner and explain the entire process, especially how the punch-out stage will work. Make it clear that the punch-out process is already built into the project timeline. Let them know that as you progress through different phases, some areas might appear incomplete—but that's completely normal. The important part is the final walkthrough, which is the homeowner's opportunity to blue-tape any items they want addressed.

And be firm: This punch-out process happens once. During this final walkthrough, the homeowner can point out anything they'd like fixed or touched up, and you'll take care of those items. After that, the expectation is that the final payment will be made. This doesn't mean you won't stand by your work—especially if there's an issue covered by a warranty. But it does mean that once the punch-out list is completed, the project is officially done, and you're not going to be chasing after endless tweaks without being paid.

The key to avoiding disputes over the punch-out process is to outline it clearly in your contract. Let the homeowner know, right from the beginning, that they'll have one chance to walk through and list any final touch-ups. Encourage them to keep a running list during the project so that nothing is missed when the time comes.

This clarity protects you from getting trapped in a cycle of endless touch-ups and unpaid work. It also helps the homeowner by giving them a clear structure for how their concerns will be addressed. When both sides understand the process, the project can finish smoothly, with everyone walking away satisfied.

OVERCOMMUNICATION

From a homeowner's perspective, they don't know what they don't know. It's up to you, as the contractor, to communicate every step of the process clearly. We've talked about this in other chapters, and it keeps coming up for a reason—overcommunication is crucial. You need to explain your process, invite questions, and keep the homeowner in the loop. Even if they're the type of person who hates confrontation, don't assume everything's fine just because they're quiet. In fact, it's often the quiet ones who hold everything in until they explode.

Take Carlos, a contractor in Oklahoma, for example. He

was working on a full home remodel for a client named Ms. Gray. Everything seemed to be going smoothly, and the project was about 90 percent complete. But out of nowhere, Ms. Gray unleashed a torrent of complaints. She went off about everything—workers not being on-site as often as she expected, slight imperfections in the tile spacing, grout lines that weren't to her liking. Every issue she had bottled up came spilling out in one heated, emotional outburst.

"You're fired, Carlos—you piece of shit!" she shouted, her voice shaking with frustration.

Carlos was blindsided. Up until that point, he thought they were doing a great job. He's a sensitive guy, and her harsh words cut deep. She still owed him $60,000, but the trust was shattered, and Carlos walked away from it. Her attorney even sent a demand letter, but when we responded with an offer to fix the remaining issues, we never heard back. Carlos managed to avoid a lawsuit, but he also had to eat the cost of the unpaid work he was rightfully owed.

The lesson? Carlos didn't take the time to set clear expectations upfront. Even though he was doing good work and cared deeply about the project, he fell short in communication.

Contractors, this is your field, your expertise. Homeowners aren't experts—they need things explained to them, often more than once. They're relying on you to guide them through the process. From their perspective, they do not understand the ins and outs of how a project comes together, and it's part of your job to keep them informed.

That's a key theme throughout this entire book. Yes, you have the skills, knowledge, and experience to handle the technical side of the work. But the other part of your job—just as important—is managing people and their expectations. Communicate well from the start, and you'll save yourself a lot of unnecessary headaches down the road.

DON'T FORGET ABOUT TIME

The punch-out process could stretch things out longer than you expected—so don't forget about time. Depending on how extensive the punch-out list is, it might even require a change order to adjust the completion date. Let's say you're at the end of the project, walking through with the homeowner, and there are a ton of small fixes that need to be addressed. Nothing major, but enough to eat up time. As the contractor, it's on you to recognize that this might push the actual completion date beyond what was originally agreed.

For example, if the project was supposed to wrap up on

September 20 but the punch-out list is going to take another ten days, you need to communicate that to the homeowner. Let them know: "Hey, I've got the punch-out list, I'll take care of everything, but it's going to take us until the end of the month to finish." At that point, you should issue a change order to formally extend the timeline. This is key—if you forget to adjust the timeline, you could end up in breach of your own contract, which is a situation you don't want to be in.

Now, homeowners might not love the idea of adding time to the schedule, especially when they're eager to be done. They might already have furniture in storage or plans that depend on a certain finish date. That's why over-communicating this timeline adjustment is so important. If you're clear upfront and let them know how long the punch-out process will take, they're less likely to get frustrated. It also ties back to protecting yourself from consequential damages—like if the delay causes them to pay for another month of storage.

WHY THE PUNCH-OUT LIST MATTERS IN COURT

Here's the thing about punch-out lists: What might seem like minor touch-ups to you can look like glaring flaws to a jury. Imagine photos of small scratches, missing mortar, or a crooked doorknob displayed in a courtroom—suddenly, those minor issues start looking like huge problems. And if the jury is mostly made up of homeowners (which it often is), they don't see it from a contractor's perspective. They see it from their own, and they don't know what they don't know.

This is why it's so crucial to put the punch-out process in your contract and take the time explaining it to your clients. If you get fired before you've had a chance to complete the punch-out, those unfinished details can paint you as a sloppy contractor who abandoned the job. The jury won't understand that you were planning to address those issues—they only see what was left undone.

We had a case like this once on a masonry project. We weren't finished yet; we'd moved on to another section but were planning to come back and handle the final touches. The homeowner didn't understand that, fired the contractor, and then those photos of missing mortar and other small imperfections ended up in front of a jury. It was a tough battle because to the jury, it looked like we'd just walked away and left the project in bad shape.

Even if you're at the end of a long project and you're tired, don't let that temptation to just walk away get the best of you. Leaving things unresolved because of a small payment dispute could come back to haunt you if it escalates into a legal battle.

When you have the punch-out process clearly written into your contract, even if you're fired or things go south before you can finish, you've got a documented plan that shows you intended to address any issues on the project. If photos of unfinished work end up in court, you can point to your contract and say, "These were items I was scheduled to take care of, but I wasn't allowed to complete the process." It's not a perfect defense, but it's much stronger than having nothing to back you up.

> **KEY TAKEAWAYS**
>
> - Have a punch-out process, and put it in your contract.
> - Take the time to explain the punch-out process to the homeowner before the contract is signed.
> - Emphasize that this process happens once, and then final payment will be due.

NO MORE SPINNING WHEELS

Never spin your wheels with a client at the end of a project again. By setting expectations early, overcommunicating throughout the job, and clearly defining the punch-out process in your contract, you can avoid the common pitfalls that trip up so many contractors.

Remember, homeowners don't always know what's happening behind the scenes. They need you to guide them through the process. Whether it's adjusting timelines with a change order or ensuring the final walkthrough is comprehensive, clear communication is your best tool for preventing disputes.

And don't forget, what might look like a minor issue to you can be blown out of proportion in a courtroom. Protect yourself by having the punch-out process in writing. If things go south, you'll have a solid defense showing you intended to finish the job properly.

At the end of the day, a smooth punch-out process isn't just about getting paid—it's about ensuring the homeowner feels satisfied, confident, and ready to recommend your work to others. When you manage this stage well, you're not just finishing a project; you're building trust, protecting your business, and setting yourself up for future success.

While this book is dedicated to the contract between you and the homeowner, there is another relationship that warrants a contract, too: with your subs, which we'll talk about next.

CHAPTER 16

BONUS CHAPTER: CONTRACTS WITH SUBS

Consider this your bonus chapter—something extra just for you. Up to this point, we've been talking about how to protect yourself in contracts with homeowners, but there's another area where contractors are often exposed and might not even realize it: subcontracting.

When you bring in subs to handle parts of a project, you're taking on a new layer of risk. Not only could you find yourself dealing with issues from the homeowner's side, but you could also end up in hot water with the subcontractors themselves.

That's why it's essential to have a separate, well-drafted contract with each of your subs. This chapter will explain why these agreements are critical and what key elements you need to include to protect yourself and your business. Whether it's clarifying responsibilities, setting clear payment terms, or outlining expectations, having everything in writing can save you from a lot of headaches down the road. This chapter is about looking out for you, the contractor, and making sure your business is covered from all angles.

WHY YOU NEED A CONTRACT WITH SUBS

Why is it so important to have a contract with your subcontractors? There are practical and legal reasons, and both fall under covering your ass.

PRACTICAL REASONS

Practically speaking, a contract helps you define the relationship and set clear expectations. You want to outline the standard of work, ensure your subs have proper insurance, and confirm they carry workers' comp for their own crew. You also need to specify that the homeowner has to approve their work before the subcontractors get paid, and the work has to meet the agreed-upon plans and specifications. If the work isn't up to standard, it's their responsibility to fix it, and they're not entitled to payment until it's done right (more on payment terms coming up).

When you bring in subcontractors, you're not just hiring extra hands; you're extending your reputation. That means you need to be clear about your standards and set expectations from the start. Even though they aren't officially part of your company, they're representing you, whether you're on-site or not.

As such, take the time to sit down with your subs and communicate your level of quality. Let them know exactly what you expect and how you want things done. If you have specific standards or methods you adhere to, make sure they understand and follow those too. This isn't just about getting the job done; it's about ensuring the work meets your company's standards every time. Educating your subcontractors on your expectations upfront will help avoid misunderstandings and maintain the quality you're known for.

Payment Terms

A key element to include in your subcontractor agreements is clear payment terms. Simply put, the sub doesn't get paid until the homeowner approves the work and pays you. This might sound straightforward, but it can get messy fast if you don't spell it out.

Think of it like managing two sets of agreements: You've got your contract with the homeowner, which outlines when and how you get paid, and then there's your contract with the sub, which should mirror that process. Your payment to the sub happens only after you've received approval and payment from the homeowner. Subcontractors might try to negotiate different terms, but you need to protect yourself.

Here's a common scenario: The subcontractor finishes their work, but the homeowner doesn't approve it. Maybe something needs to be fixed, or it doesn't meet the agreed-upon specs. The sub, however, still expects to be paid, putting you in a tough spot. Without a clear agreement, you're left with nothing to stand on except your word. But if your contract states that the sub's payment is contingent on homeowner approval, you have leverage. You can say, "I want to pay you, but we need to get this work approved first, and that's your responsibility."

The process is simple: Step one, the sub finishes their work. Step two, the homeowner approves it. Step three, the sub gets paid. This system ensures that everything is completed to the homeowner's satisfaction before you hand over any money, keeping you out of a sticky situation where you're paying for unfinished or unsatisfactory work.

LEGAL REASONS

From a legal standpoint, having a subcontract protects you from being entangled in potentially messy situations. For instance, if someone gets injured on the job, things can get complicated fast. Without a contract, a subcontractor or their employee might try to claim they're your employee, which could lead to you being sued. If they succeed, your workers' comp doesn't cover them because they're not technically your employee, and you're stuck defending yourself in court. But with a clear subcontract in place, you can prove they're not your employee, saving you from a potential legal headache.

There's also the risk that a subcontractor's injured worker could try to sue the homeowner. If you have it clearly spelled out in the subcontract that the subcontractor must provide workers' comp, you're protecting yourself and your client from this possibility.

Another thing to keep in mind: If you carry workers' comp insurance, your insurer will audit your books every year. They'll look at everyone you paid, and if there's no subcontract, they'll assume those individuals are your employees and bump up your premium. I had a client who learned this the hard way. After an audit, he got hit with a $50,000 bill because the insurer assumed he had a bunch of new employees. Luckily, he had subcontracts for those folks and was able to prove they weren't his employees, reducing his bill significantly. Without those contracts, he would've been stuck paying that full amount.

Additional Insured

A key step in managing your subcontractor relationships is adding yourself as an "additional insured" on their insurance policy. You might already have a contract that requires proof of insurance from your subs, and that's great, but you also need to make sure they add you as an additional insured.

Why? Because—and this is important—*only the insured party can file an insurance claim.*

I had a case once where a subcontractor worked in a wine cellar, and during the job, he accidentally set off the sprinkler system. No one was around to turn it off, and the place ended up flooding over the weekend, causing extensive damage.

Now, this is exactly what general liability (GL) insurance is for, but the policy would be on the subcontractor, not you. The homeowner has a contract with you, so their claim would go to you. If you're listed as an additional insured on the sub's policy, you can file the claim directly. If you're not, however, only the subcontractor can do that, and there's no guarantee he will—or that you'll even be able to track him down, especially if this happens years later.

In our case, thankfully my client was added to this subcontractor's insurance and we were able to file the claim. If he wasn't, he would have been on the hook for those damages (meaning he would have had to file on his own insurance).

Adding yourself as an additional insured means you don't have to rely on the sub to handle claims. You can take matters into your own hands, protect your business, and avoid chasing after someone else to fix a problem.

Sheesh, you may be thinking. *This sounds like a lot.*

And it is! But don't worry—you can streamline the whole process with a Master Subcontract.

SIMPLIFYING WITH A MASTER SUBCONTRACT

A master subcontract allows you to have a consistent set of terms and conditions that apply to *all* your subcontractors, making sure everyone knows the rules upfront. This is a comprehensive agreement that covers all the legal requirements—insurance, workers' comp, quality standards, and payment terms—so you only have to sign it once, and it applies to every job you do with that sub in the future.

A master subcontract streamlines the process by eliminating the need to draft a new contract for each project. Instead, for each job, you just issue a *work order* that falls under the umbrella of the master subcontract. This makes things easier for both you and your subs, and ensures everyone is clear on what's expected.

Using a master subcontract isn't just about streamlining paperwork; it's about covering your bases. For example, if a subcontractor's worker gets injured on your site, and you don't have a clear agreement, they might try to claim they're your employee. That could land you in serious legal trouble. But with a signed subcontract in place, you can prove they're not your responsibility, saving you from a potential lawsuit and hefty legal fees.

Having this agreement also ensures your subs carry their own workers' comp insurance, which protects you from claims if one of their employees gets hurt on the job. And remember, your insurance company will audit your books at the end of the year. If they see payments to subcontractors without signed contracts, they might classify them as your employees, bumping up your workers' comp premium. With a master subcontract, you can easily show that these folks are not your employees.

TIMES HAVE CHANGED

The construction industry isn't what it was thirty years ago, when you could rely on a handshake and a promise. Even if you've worked with the same subcontractors for decades, you need to protect yourself with a written contract. Business practices have changed, and so have the risks. Even if a sub is your buddy and has done good work for you in the past, you never know when something might go wrong, and without a contract, your business could be exposed.

A master subcontract helps you manage these risks effectively. At first, this might sound like a lot to manage, but a well-drafted master subcontract simplifies things. It lays out the rules, sets the standards, and ensures that everyone knows what's expected. Plus, you can include additional clauses, like prohibiting the homeowner from hiring your subs directly or requiring approval for any extra work before it's done, preventing unwanted surprises on your invoices.

> **KEY TAKEAWAYS**
>
> - Always use a written subcontract; it is a vital component to CYA.
> - Set clear payment terms.
> - Add yourself as additional insured.
> - Streamline the process with a master subcontract that only has to be signed once.

NOT JUST ABOUT EXTRA HELP

When it comes to subcontracting, it's not just about getting extra help; it's about protecting your business and maintaining your reputation. Having a solid contract with your subs is essential for setting clear expectations, avoiding legal headaches, and ensuring everyone knows where they stand. Whether it's making sure you're listed as an additional insured on their policy, outlining strict payment terms, or using a master subcontract to streamline your agreements, these steps can save you from a lot of trouble down the road.

A well-crafted master subcontract can simplify this process, giving you peace of mind knowing that your projects are protected. So don't leave things to chance. Take the time to get these contracts right, and you'll not only safeguard your business but also build stronger, more reliable partnerships with your subcontractors.

CONCLUSION

Throughout this book, we've covered the essentials of protecting yourself as a contractor, from the first handshake to the final payment. It all starts with a solid, written contract. Clear agreements set the tone for the project, manage expectations, and provide that crucial CYA (cover your ass) protection.

But a contract alone isn't enough—trust your instincts, and don't be afraid to walk away from a potential client if something doesn't feel right.

We've emphasized the importance of defining a detailed scope of work, so there's no confusion about what's included. We also dove into change orders, payment terms, scheduling, and planning for the unexpected—key strategies that keep your projects on track and your cash flow smooth. Having clear provisions for cancellation, standards, and warranties ensures you're covered if things don't go as planned.

Whether it's dealing with disputes, setting up a punch-out process, or managing subcontractors, the key message is simple: Clear communication and solid contracts are your best defense. They help you avoid misunderstandings, keep projects running smoothly, and ensure you get paid for the hard work you do.

MORE THAN JUST LEGAL PROTECTION

If there's one thing I hope you take away from this book, it's that contracts are about so much more than just legal protection. Sure, they're important for keeping you covered, but a well-crafted contract is also a powerful tool for building successful relationships with homeowners. It's a communication tool—a way to set clear expectations, avoid misunderstandings, and pave the path for smoother projects and happier clients. When you get it right, a contract isn't just a piece of paper; it's the foundation for your success.

And don't be intimidated by the process. There's no secret, special language you need to master. Your contract should reflect your experience, your business, and the specific requirements of the state you work in. It doesn't have to be complicated—just clear, straightforward, and tailored to your needs.

This book gives you everything you need to draft your own contracts, so go out and do it! But if you'd rather have someone else take care of it, I'm here to help.

I've developed a unique system that offers flat-fee, five-business-day turnaround for customized construction contracts, covering all fifty states. As far as I know, I'm the only one doing it this way, and I'm confident in saying it's the best approach out there. You can find others who will do construction contracts, but if they aren't construction lawyers, the results might fall short. Even other construction lawyers don't offer the speed and flat-fee structure I do, which means if you need a contract fast, my process is designed to deliver.

Visit www.thecromeenslawfirm.com if you'd like to learn more. I also invite you to call for a free consultation.

Lastly, I hope this book helps you recognize your value. Too often, contractors sell themselves short, undercutting their own worth. The work you do is important—it requires skill, experience, and a lot of hard-earned knowledge. You deserve to be paid fairly for it.

With the right contract, you can be more confident, stand

your ground, and make sure your contracts reflect just how valuable your services are.

Just don't forget to *trust your gut*.

ABOUT THE AUTHOR

KARALYNN CROMEENS is a published author, seasoned managing partner, and devoted leader who has built a powerhouse team at the Cromeens Law Firm, PLLC. With over seventeen years of experience in construction, real estate, and business law, Karalynn understands the unique challenges contractors face daily. She's passionate about protecting the businesses her clients have built and serving as a lifelong partner in their success.

Karalynn's journey began with a Bachelor of Science in Criminal Justice from Carroll College, followed by earning her Juris Doctorate from South Texas College of Law in 2004. After gaining experience as an associate attorney at the Law Office of J. Tomkins, she founded the Cromeens Law Firm in 2006, where she's since filed over a thousand lawsuits to foreclose or remove mechanic's liens, several of which have gone to jury trial. Under her leadership, the firm has grown tremendously, and she continues to mentor her team while providing clients with innovative legal strategies to safeguard their rights.

A trailblazer in the construction industry, Karalynn is on a mission to educate subcontractors about the importance of fair subcontracts and understanding lien and collections rights. This mission inspired her to author *Quit Getting Screwed: Understanding and Negotiating the Subcontract* and *Quit Getting Stiffed: A Texas Contractor's Guide to Collections and Lien Rights,* as well as to create The Subcontractor Institute, an online resource for subcontractors. She also hosts the popular *Quit Getting Screwed* podcast, offering free, practical education to contractors nationwide.

When she's not empowering contractors or mentoring her team, Karalynn enjoys spending time with her husband, Brad, and their three daughters—Lily, Holly, and Jessy.

www.ingramcontent.com/pod-product-compliance
Lightning Source LLC
Chambersburg PA
CBHW030519080526
44586CB00011B/249